# the life and times of
# ROSIE·THE·RIVETER

# ...fe and times of ROSIE · THE · RIVETER

"One of the ten best films of the year."
*VILLAGE VOICE*

**Domestic. Shop girl. Waitress. Cook** . . . Those were the jobs for women in the 1930's — when they could get work. Suddenly the U.S. entry into World War II created an unprecedented demand for new workers. Notions of what was proper work for women changed overnight. Thousands of posters and billboards appeared calling on women to "Do the Job He Left Behind." Rosie the Riveter was born — the symbol of working women during World War II.

After whirlwind training, women found themselves doing "men's work" and they did it so well that production levels rose despite the military call-up of millions of male workers. Women discovered a new sense of pride and dignity in their work. Their earnings leapt upwards. Many joined unions and found substantial new benefits from labor representation. And for the first time in history, black women gained entry into major industrial plants.

When the war was over, Rosie wanted to stay. But neither the structure of the American economy nor the dominant view of women's place in society sustained such hopes.

The story is told by the women themselves — five former "Rosies" who movingly recall their histories working in Detroit, Los Angeles, New York and San Francisco during the war. Their testimony is interwoven with rare archival recruitment films, stills, posters, ads and music from the period which contrast their experiences with the popular legend and mythology of Rosie the Riveter. □

"**I recommend this film!** We are shocked into realizing how the media can shape our attitudes, and how contemporary media can still, in a more subtle fashion, shape what we think about ourselves."

James M. Wall, Ed., CHRISTIAN CENTURY

"**A superb film** on the experience of female workers in America during World War II. The film brilliantly exposes the hypocrisy that underlay American chauvinism during the war . . . a remarkable demonstration of the manipulative power of propaganda."

Bruce McCabe, BOSTON SUNDAY GLOBE

"**Warm, engaging and poignant.** The film has that Studs Terkel-like ability to discover the extraordinary in seemingly ordinary people. Terrific."

LA TIMES

"**Does a remarkable job** of revealing the traditional concept of men's and women's roles . . . a valuable, compelling and entertaining piece of modern American history."

LOUISVILLE TIMES

"**Masterfully told.** Despite the time gap, many of the women's remembrances ring familiar: constant pressure to produce more; locked out for organizing a union; told to "make do" with poor safety conditions; barred from a washroom for being black. Both men and women will find this fascinating, thought-provoking and entertaining."

UAW SOLIDARITY

## A one-hour, 16mm, color documentary

*Produced and Directed by:* Connie Field     *Edited by:* Lucy Massie Phenix, Connie Field
*Associate Producers:* Bonnie Bellow, Ellen Geiger, Lorraine Kahn, Jane Scantlebury
*Associate Director:* Lorraine Kahn     *Assistant Editor:* Robert Epstein
*Presented by:* Clarity Educational Productions
*Funded in part by:* National Endowment for the Humanities

*For rental and sale information, contact:*
*Clarity Educational Productions*
*P.O. Box 315, Franklin Lakes, N.J. 07417  (201) 891-8240*

# the life and times of
# ROSIE·THE·RIVETER

## The Story of Three Million Working Women During World War II

by Miriam Frank, Marilyn Ziebarth
and Connie Field

Supported by the National Endowment for the Humanities

Clarity Educational Productions
Emeryville, California
1982

FRONT COVER: Workers leave a Richmond, California, shipyard at the end of a long shift. *Dorothea Lange Collection, Oakland Museum*

BACK COVER: Most women eagerly signed up for well-paying jobs in defense industries. *Marjory Collins, Library of Congress.* Aided by unions and progressive black organizations, black women, including this riveting and bucking team at Douglas Aircraft, moved into war plant jobs. *Office of War Information, Library of Congress*

Grateful acknowledgment is made for permission to reprint this previously published material:

South End Press: Excerpts from *I Looked Over Jordan* by Ernie Brill (1980) and *Indignant Heart* by Charles Denby (second printing, 1978). Reprinted by permission of the publisher.

The MacMillan Company: Excerpt from *The Dollmaker* by Harriet Arnow (1949). Reprinted by permission of the publisher.

ISBN # 09607334-1-8 (Educator's Edition).
ISBN # 09607334-0-XX (Reader's Edition)

Clarity Educational Productions, Inc.
4560 Horton Street
Emeryville, California 94608

The views expressed in this book are those of the authors and do not necessarily represent those of the National Endowment for the Humanities.

Typeset by Archetype, Berkeley, California. Printed by George Lithograph Company, San Francisco.

# ACKNOWLEDGEMENTS

*This study guide was prepared with the support of a grant from the National Endowment for the Humanities and the cooperation of the following organizations:*

Workers Education Local 189
United Food and Commercial Workers (Retail Clerks), Local 1100, San Francisco
International Brotherhood of Teamsters, Local 315, Contra Costa County, California
Walter Reuther Library of Labor and Urban Affairs, Wayne State University
Amalgamated Clothing and Textile Workers' Union, Threads Project (NEH) and Local 1781, Charlotte, North Carolina
United Auto Workers, Dave Miller Retiree Center, Local 163, and Reg. Women's Comm., Detroit
Alexander Crummell Church, Detroit
Hard Hat Women of Cleveland
National Association of Office Workers (Working Women), Cleveland and Pittsburgh
Displaced Homemakers, Cuyahoga Community College, Cleveland, Ohio, Tanawanda, New York, and Fredonia, New York
Service Employees International Union, Local 585, Blawnox, Pennsylvania
National Congress of Neighborhood Women, Pittsburgh
Cornell Institute of Labor and Industrial Relations, Buffalo, New York
Austin Unitarian Church, Austin, Illinois
United Steelworkers of America, Local 1010 and District 31 Women's Caucus, East Chicago and Gary, Indiana
Walter Reuther Senior Citizens' Center, Detroit
Highlander Center, New Market, Tennessee
American Friends Service Committee, Coburn, Virginia
Theology in the Americas, Labor Task Force
Dickenson County (Virginia) Food Coop
International Union of Electrical Workers, Local 748, Jefferson City, Tennessee
Knoxville Women's Center
Fourth and Gill Neighborhood Assoc., Knoxville
Brown Lung Association

Vote Task Force, Charlotte, North Carolina
Southerners for Economic Justice, Greenville, South Carolina
Bernal Heights Neighborhood Association, San Francisco

*The following individuals have contributed to the making of this study guide by testing drafts of the material with their organizations, by contributing research, or by consulting with us in the planning and development of the manuscript:*

Marguerite Adelman, William Adelman, Wanita Allen, Ronald Alpern, Karen Anderson, Lisa Anderson, Betty Arnth, Elizabeth Balanoff, Gladys Belcher, Brenda Bell, Susan Porter Benson, Addy Brodsky, Grace Lee Boggs, Evelyn Bonder, Melba Boyd, Charlotte Brody, David Brody, Bill Bryce, Glenora Cameron, D'Ann Campbell, Lyn Childs, Barbara Christian, Marvin Ciporen, Alan Clive, Sue Cobble, Jaime Cohen, Cita Cook, Vicky Creed, Howard Dratch, Nuala Dresher, Tim Dzierba, Enid Eckstein, Rebecca Eckstein, Barbara Ellis, Bosanka Evosovic, LuJean Fleron, Nancy Gabin, Ellen Geiger, Cynthia Gerney, Jessie Glaberman, Martin Glaberman, Sherna Gluck, Lyn Goldfarb, Dorothy Haener, Rosemary Hannah, John Hare, Susan Hartman, Maureen Honey, Myles Horton, Gloria House, Jim Jacobs, Lorraine Kahn, Virginia Kaiser, Rebecca Klatch, Carol Kurtz, Vicky Lebovicz, Karen Liedtke, Leon Litwack, Joyce Maupin, Ruth Meyerowitz, Ruth Milkman, David K. Miller, Christine Noschese, Victoria Ortiz, Sandy Pope, Donald Prange, Leslie Rainey, Bernice Reagon, Braudy Richardson, Janet Ridgway, Cheryl Robinson, June Rostan, Vidya Sendra, Sarah Slaughter, Tish Sommers, Syl Sampson, Jane Scantlebury, Dagmar Schultz, Karen Beck Skold, Joan Smith, Milo Smith, Suzi Suafai, Joycelyn Thompson, Loren Thompson, Sue Thrasher, Sheila Tobias, Theresa Tollini, Joan Ellen Trey, Rosemary Trump, George Tselos, Edie Van Horn, Pam Weinstein, Lola Weixel, Barbara Wertheimer, Rebecca Wilson, Charles Wolfenbarger, Margaret Wright, Christine Zupcik.

# CONTENTS

(Facing Page)
End of the shift at a Buffalo, New York, steel plant in 1943. *Marjory Collins, Library of Congress*

# ROSIE THE RIVETER— A GENERATION LATER

Former welder Lola Weixel, the film's "Rosie the Riveter" from Brooklyn, and I must be almost the same age. Watching Lola look out from the stage at Lincoln Center across the sea of mostly young faces following the premiere in 1980 of *The Life and Times of Rosie the Riveter* at the New York Film Festival, I believe we must have shared some of the same thoughts. What, she probably wondered, would the film say to young people 40 years after the outbreak of a war they never regarded as "the" war, as we did. They had laughed at the propaganda of the newsreels luring women into war industries and then urging them to go home again when the war was over. Would the younger audience understand how the key issues in the film are much the same as those facing women in the workforce today? The warm ovation that Lola received that night, I think, testified to the success of the film at bringing that message to a new generation of postwar women.

Some months later in Michigan, I heard Wanita Allen, the film's "Rosie" from Detroit, talk to labor union women following a showing of the film. Although the audience was older and several women had been war workers themselves, most recalled the event through child's eyes, if at all. Would these viewers, I reflected, see the film only as a salute to the past? Or would they recognize how much progress working women have made since that time and how their roles in their unions have changed today? Again, I saw that the film spoke clearly to them. The standing ovation given Wanita was one of the most moving demonstrations of respect I have ever witnessed. "We understand. You paved the way for our gain. We thank you," the audience said.

In just over a year, more than a million viewers in the United States and abroad have seen *The Life and Times of*

Lola Weixel helps scout locations for the film, *The Life and Times of Rosie the Riveter. Connie Field*

*Rosie the Riveter.* Now, we are fortunate to have this book which builds on the film's brief stories of five women who worked in war production plants and what happened to them after the war. History is an ongoing process of rediscovery, and in focusing on the role played by women in the war effort, the book's photographs, oral histories, and essays put women back into the history of America during the 1940's.

For women workers, the decades since the war have marked rapid change, and today more than half of all adult women are in the workforce. For the first time, women bring to their jobs the same educational level as men (an average of 12.8 years) and the same motivation to use their education and talents. More than one in every six union members are women. Although society sometimes still portrays women's economic contributions as marginal or ex-

Wanita Allen (center) and Beulah Work being interviewed by Lenore Goldman at the Detroit Rosie the Riveter reunion. *Reg McGee*

Margaret Wright during the filming.
*Connie Field*

pendable, women are clearly in the workforce to stay. They are frequently heads of families or share major responsibility for supporting their families, and they work for the same reason men do—economic need. Forty years have brought a new consciousness among women.

Today, the wartime era's concept of equal pay for equal work is being extended to equal pay for work of comparable value. Because women still earn an average of 62¢ for every dollar earned by men for full-time work, jobs traditionally considered "women's work" must be revalued to close the wage gap caused by sex segregation at the workplace.

Another primary event of the decades since the war has been the struggle for better pay, conditions, and jobs by minority women who now are a substantial number of all clerical, government, professional, and technical workers. In turn, the Civil Rights movement, the women's movement and the labor movement have often campaigned cooperatively to win legislation that has opened skilled blue-collar trades to women and minorities, protected all workers from job hazards, and gained job rights for pregnant women.

But now, many of the rights women have painstakingly won—access to education, to housing and credit, and the right to choose when to bear children—are under attack. Newspapers and magazines suggest that the country's high unemployment rate is caused by women entering the workforce, that working women have more divorces and breakdowns under job stresses, that juvenile delinquency is the result of women working outside the home, and that sexual harassment is a problem invited by women.

It is no coincidence that the current administration in Washington, D.C., is systematically curtailing affirmative action guidelines for women and minorities, and is cutting back on child care and medical services, food stamps, and welfare programs. These programs especially benefit the poor, many of whom are women. It is women, too, who will be forced to forego paid employment to care for children and elderly adults who are losing the minimal assistance on which they have depended. Thousands of other women will never find work because public service jobs such as those funded through the Comprehensive Employment and Training Act (CETA) have been abolished.

Gladys Belcher during a newspaper interview after the release of the film.
*Richmond* (California) *Independent*

Lyn Childs at the opening of the film at the 1980 San Francisco Film Festival.
*Kathy Sloane*

Full employment is as important an issue today as it was after World War II when 3¼ million women were no longer needed by war industries and 14 million veterans returned to civilian life. Today, the nation's unemployment rate again runs over 7 percent, and the same need exists for a socially responsible government that will ensure all its citizens the opportunity to work.

One clear difference between Rosie the Riveter and to-day's working woman is the tools she has at hand to maintain her economic gains. Labor organizations in particular offer an outstanding opportunity for women. Almost 7 million women belong to unions or associations where they are learning how to work within the union structure, gaining organizing experience, and developing leadership skills, transferable to myriad other organizations.

Many women have joined the Coalition of Labor Union Women (CLUW), a national organization that brings labor movement women together to achieve political, legislative and union affirmative action goals. On another front, clerical workers, over 95 percent of whom are women, are organizing their offices through such groups as Working Women—The National Association of Office Workers, and District 925 of the Service Employees International Union.

Women are participating forcefully in work, union, and community life. Women's caucuses in workplaces, education and women's departments in labor organizations, the educational resources offered through university labor extension programs, and union training schools also help develop women's leadership potential and focus on issues confronting all women who work outside the home. The message in *The Life and Times of Rosie the Riveter* and this companion book is that women's gains in the 1940's were lost for a generation because the tools to sustain the movement were not at hand. As the challenge to women's rights mounts, each of us must pledge that what working women have achieved will not be relinquished. Matching the courage of Rosie the Riveter, we will succeed.

*Barbara Mayer Wertheimer,*
*New York State School of Industrial and Labor Relations,*
*Cornell University, New York City*

# WOMEN AND WORK, WOMEN AND WAR

*Women are working only to win the war and will return to their home duties after the war is won. They will look on this period as an interlude, just as their men who have been called to service will consider military duties as an interlude. The women are like Cincinnatus, who left his plow to save Rome and then returned to his plow. Women will always be women.*

—Betty Allie,
State Workmen's Compensation Official

Most Americans remember Rosie the Riveter as the plucky housewife who served her country on the homefront during World War II. For "the duration," as the war years were known, she patriotically left her comfortable home to work in her town's defense plant. At war's end, the myth goes, she eagerly shed her overalls and resumed her natural job of keeping house and raising children.

While this nostalgic image describes some women war workers, it ignores the lives of at least two out of three of the women who entered wartime defense plants. These women welders and riveters had already worked outside their homes for wages. They had been former service and domestic workers, low-skilled, poorly paid factory workers in predominantly all-women's industries, such as garment- and pottery-making, and agricultural laborers. Many were minority women and single mothers. Others were fresh from school or

family. First entering the workforce during the war, many would continue—out of necessity or choice—to work outside their homes for the rest of their lives.

When the war ended, in fact, few of these women chose to leave their factory jobs. Instead, they were laid off or fired. Forced out of skilled, well-paying work, most did not "retire" but instead took the next job that they could find. Like generations of women before them (and the more than 50 percent of today's women who are members of the paid workforce), they worked primarily because they had to support themselves and their families.

Women have always worked outside their homes in the United States. It was the agricultural labor of slaves—among them black women—which made the South rich before the Revolutionary War. Women traditionally made cloth and clothing in the home, and when these crafts were industrialized in the early nine-

(Facing Page)  Minority women formed one-fifth of the wartime industrial workforce in some cities.
*Schomburg Center Collection, New York Public Library*

teenth century, it was women and children who became the nation's first factory workers. In the decades to follow, female immigrants staffed laundries and garment-making and cigar-rolling factories. They also waited on wealthy people in hotels, restaurants, and private homes. During World War I, women took over producing the nation's food, and for the first time they moved into heavy industrial jobs in munitions plants and other defense industries. Like the next generation of World War II women, they were dismissed on Armistice Day, 1918.

Even during the great Depression of the 1930's, the percentage of women working in the paid labor force continued to rise. While heavy industrial production declined and male workers lost jobs, some ten million women—22 percent of the workforce—continued to find employment, but in unskilled, low-wage jobs.

Foundry worker Ruth Wolf, who was then living in Ohio, recalls:

> The depression was hard for me. My husband was gone for three years; he had lost his job and had just hit the road. So it was just me and my children. I saw the time when we ate everything in the house for breakfast, and I didn't know what we would have to eat for the rest of the day. There was no work, not even housework. But one day my daughter came rushing in the house. She was running down the stairs to tell me something, and she got almost to the last stair and she slipped and fell and was screaming, "Mother, mother, you've got a job! You've got a job! They've called you to come back to work!" The pottery factory had called me back to work. It was 1932. But pottery wages were a sweatshop affair. I was making $14 a week. I hired someone to come in and take care of my kids. It wasn't hard to find someone who was in even worse condition than I was!

Domestic service meant long hours, no overtime pay, and working conditions set entirely by the employing family. "We were called 'kitchen mechanics' and we got every other Thursday off, and Sunday, maybe, if we were very good" (Margaret Wright, ammunitions worker).
*Library of Congress*

Before the war, many black women could find only seasonal, low-paid, and mostly unorganized jobs in agriculture.
*National Archives*

Southern textile mills like this one in Greene County, Georgia, manufactured cotton cloth for military use. Despite lucrative cost-plus contracts, mill owners kept wages low in this non-union industry. *Jack Delano, Library of Congress*

The outbreak of war virtually ended the nation's grave problem of 10 million unemployed workers. While the manufacture of military goods had already begun, the 1941 attack on Pearl Harbor shifted the new war economy into high gear. Private industries built new plants, converted old ones, and expanded production and profits under the "cost plus" contract system. By this agreement, the army, navy, or another branch of the federal government generously paid the cost of private industry's raw materials, labor, machinery acquisitions, and conversion of production systems, plus a fixed profit. As a result, munitions production increased 225 percent during 1941 alone, while corporate profits during the war soared from $6.4 to $10.8 billion. "If you are going to war or to prepare for war in a capitalist country, you have got to let business make money out of the process, or business won't work," Secretary of War Henry Stimson observed with surprising candor.

Active involvement by the government in civilian life also characterized the new war economy of the 1940's. Boards consisting of government officials and business leaders set economic policy. A government labor board controlled workers' wage demands while the Office of Price Administration tried to control prices, which nonetheless rose substantially. The War Production Board determined what goods could be manufactured, and the government also rationed food, gasoline, and consumer goods. In essence, the country moved to a planned economy because efficient use of labor manpower and raw materials became critically important to the war effort. New legal regulations controlled civilian activities, including the rights of workers to move from job to job, and millions of men were drafted into the armed services.

### Building the New Wartime Workforce

As men were called up and the need for war goods increased, people who had been considered "marginal" workers by employers— women, all minorities, older people, even the disabled and blind—became the targets of vigorous recruitment campaigns. Industries that had once employed only white males were persuaded by government planners and government-issued pamphlets to relieve their manpower shortage by taking on these new workers. Getting a defense job was still far from easy, and some women had to fight to get hired.

Eighteen million women were in the workforce during World War II, some six million of them for the first time. While the majority worked in traditional women's occupations, three million were working in defense industries. The number of women in heavy manufacturing increased some 460 percent, and the nature of their work, as well as the size of their paychecks, changed just as dramatically.

Women learned the new industrial skills quickly. "Almost overnight," observed Mary Anderson of the Department of Labor Women's Bureau, "women were reclassified by industrialists from a marginal to a basic labor supply for munitions making."

Women gather at the Boeing Hiring Hall in Seattle in 1942. They responded to employee recruitment drives because the pay in aircraft plants was much higher than in light manufacturing or domestic work.
*Carol Eyerman Collection*

Lengthy job apprenticeships were suspended to meet the demands of wartime production, and women were trained as welders, press operators, and riveters in a matter of weeks. *National Archives*

This sudden move into industrial work markedly affected women's personal sense of themselves. Former war worker Lola Weixel recalls the enthusiasm the women welders shared:

> We were going to get in on the ground floor and be welders for ever and ever. It was almost an art, as well as a skill. It was a very beautiful kind of work. At the end of the day I always felt I had accomplished something. There was a product. There was something to be seen.

Jumping into whirlwind training programs that taught them to do "men's work" practically overnight, women welcomed the opportunity for the jobs—and the good salaries that went with them.

> I took the job because, number one, I needed work; number two, I'd had bad experience in jobs before where I hadn't felt any pride in the kind of work I was doing; number three, there was a war on and the people were all enthused about helping out in every way they could.
> —Lyn Childs, shipburner

Because most big war production plants were unionized, many women experienced for the first time some of the benefits of being part of an organized work force. Minority women, who formed 10 to 19 percent of the female workers in major war production centers like New York, Los Angeles, and Detroit, also shared in the improved way of life. Ammunitions worker Margaret Wright remembers that in spite of the overt racism experienced by many women in the plants

> It was still a good time for me because having worked for a dollar a day or ten dollars at the most, it was good to be getting 100 dollars, because I had never made that much money.

War-related industries attracted the largest numbers of new women workers, but women also entered government service and office work in record numbers. Garment and electrical shops continued to employ women, as they had before the war, but on defense contracts making uniforms or military equipment. Women took over shipbuilding, aircraft, and weapons manufacturing operations as welders, riveters, and machine workers. Other manufacturing industries which produced communications equipment, small arms, and rubber goods also added women to their workforce.

Enormous as these changes were, they did not signal the achievement of economic or social equality. Discrimination on the job still persisted, and with few exceptions, women did not receive equal pay, an issue which the unions

Shipyards on the East and West coasts, such as Baltimore's Bethlehem Shipyard, employed thousands of workers to construct enormous battleships. "When we finished one of these beautiful ships, it was an inspiring, thrilling thing" (Lyn Childs, shipburner). *Arthur Siegel, Library of Congress*

These women did pneumatic chipping at the Marin Shipyards in Sausalito, California. *National Archives*

often emphasized. General Motors paid women less by substituting categories of "heavy" and "light" for those of "male" and "female." In many other plants, women were placed in separate job classifications such as "helper trainee" instead of "mechanic learner," and accordingly were paid less. In addition, women were rarely promoted to supervisor status.

### Disbanding the Hidden Army

Despite the skills and economic status gained by women in the industrial work force, they remained part of what a wartime government film called the nation's "hidden army." This army was drafted to meet the wartime emergency, and, as women found out when the war ended, the troops of that hidden army could be just as quickly decommissioned when the economy no longer needed them in those jobs.

Accordingly, when industry reconverted to peacetime production in 1945—a process that within one year saw 3¼ million women out of 18 million in the workforce leave their jobs voluntarily or involuntarily—some 500,000 women never found work again. By 1950, the number of women in the labor force was again equal to that of the war years (and has risen steadily since), but the nature of the work that women were allowed to do was for the most part confined to sex-stereotyped jobs which paid substantially less than war work.

Wartime practices of keeping separate seniority lists for males, females, whites, and blacks, as well as the classification of jobs as male or female, further hurt the overwhelming majority of women who needed to keep working. In the end, women were laid off at a rate 75 percent higher than men, and the results were devastating. As Ada Habermehl remembers, "One afternoon just before the war ended, they laid off 108 of us. You never heard so many women crying in all your life."

When the United Auto Workers (UAW) asked its women members in 1944, "If a job is available, will you continue to work outside the home after the war?", 85 percent of the women answered, "Yes." This figure included a full 100 percent of the UAW women who were widows, 99 percent of the single women, and 69 percent of the married women. Another end-of-the-war survey of laid-off women workers in Detroit showed that 72 percent of them wanted work but couldn't find any.

> Ford had 40,000 employees during the war and 18,000 were women. When the war was over, they tried their darndest to get rid of the women. They said women were unstable, that we'd been absent too much, that we had our kids to look after. In my case they said I was too fat! Ford went from 18,000 to 2,000 women after they'd hired back in '46.
> —Edna Artman, riveter

The "hidden army" was clearly unwanted.

Unemployment proved particularly debilitating to women who had enjoyed their industrial jobs.

> When you're unemployed the days stretch out. Each hour is the same. In the plant there was organization in your life. We made transistors. One woman kept the little things we made around her dresser mirror like prom souvenirs.
> —Grace Lee Boggs, electrical worker

Some of these unemployed women refused jobs at lower rates of pay and tried to find skilled industrial work. Others were trapped by legal rulings such as a Michigan law which ordered that if a woman refused a job at a lower rate of pay, or would not or could not because of state law, work the third shift (usually 11 p.m. to 7 a.m.), she could not receive unemployment compensation. (Third-shift work was permitted for women who worked in typical women's occupations—waitresses in restaurants or night-duty hospital nurses and aides.)

The return of some 14 million mostly male veterans to the civilian labor force increased the difficulty women had in keeping industrial jobs. In anticipation of the problems of reintegrating the veterans, a Full Employment

Two young women, perhaps sisters, weld ships at the Bethlehem Fairfield Shipyard in Baltimore in 1943. *Arthur Siegel, Library of Congress*

Act (the Kilgore-Murray bill) was introduced into Congress in 1944 to broaden benefits and retrain workers. The bill received wide support from labor and women's organizations and from government agencies, but it was defeated again and again in Congress in the coming years. Although the government continued to take some responsibility for the employment of veterans, the needs of women and minority men were ignored. There was little effort by government to plan a rational reconversion to a peacetime economy.

Women working in heavy industry expected to lose their jobs to those returning veterans who had higher seniority. Veterans had been given "super seniority" over other workers, which meant that soldiers accumulated seniority while they were in the service.

What women were not prepared for was the

widespread discrimination against them when they tried to find other industrial jobs or to hold on to seniority in their former workplaces. They soon learned that men who were not even veterans would be given preference over women in the competition for the remaining skilled jobs. "I knew the job would terminate when the war was over," remembers Gladys Belcher.

> So I went to school after work for four hours so that when I got out of there, I could get a job welding. They were needing welders at Mare Island [navy shipyard]. So I took my card and all my credentials and I laid my papers on the desk. He said, "If you was a man, we'd hire you, but we can't hire you, you're a woman."

While full and equal employment in peacetime proved to be only a wartime fiction, Lola Weixel and her co-workers shed their post-war optimism with the greatest of reluctance:

> We believed that the economy was going to burgeon. It would be a splendid. We would rebuild the cities. We would do all these things because before the war we didn't have all these skilled people. But now we had. It would be time to do all the good and beautiful things for America because fascism was destroyed.

### Looking for Work Again

In part, war workers were victims of the nation's own wartime propaganda that raised expectations about post-war prosperity. Amid predictions that helicopters would be as common as family cars, women modestly anticipated that they would somehow be able to earn a good living in the post-war years.

Instead, highly paid industrial jobs were reserved preferentially for male workers, even those without veteran status or seniority. As a result, women were forced back to low-wage jobs in light manufacturing, or to kitchen and hotel service. Sometimes they were represented in these jobs by unions such as the Hotel, Motel and Restaurant Employees or the Amalgamated Clothing Workers of America, but often these jobs were not unionized and the work had low social status.

Welder Gladys Belcher's experience of taking extensive training yet not being able to get anything but kitchen work—a job she held for the next 17 years—was common among former war workers:

> You have a lot of responsibility, especially a widow woman, a lone woman. My children had to be taken care of, and I'd bought a little home. It had to be paid for. I had to get a job somewhere, somehow. I know that's what I was thinking about when I left there. I got a job in a restaurant working in the kitchen. Hot hard work. Heavy lifting. It was a lot harder than working in the shipyard and a lot less pay.

For many women the war years proved to be some of the best years of their working lives. For the first time large numbers of women were paid a decent wage for their labor, were able to produce products which could be seen, and were represented by unions which offered some protection on the job. The popular support accorded the war effort helped women feel that they were working for something much larger than themselves and that their work was crucial to the well-being of the nation. After the war, although they wanted to continue to earn a decent living as members of the skilled industrial labor force, changes in economic opportunities and the revived notion of women's "proper place" combined to sabotage their future chances of getting good jobs. This legacy of limiting women to certain kinds of jobs has haunted women workers ever since. □

Celia Sapersteen Yanish. *Connie Field*

## "I loved that job because I produced something."

*Machinist Celia Yanish and foundry worker Ruth Wolf were among the first women workers in World War II production plants in the United States. Although they were delighted to learn a trade and to be producing goods essential to the war effort, they had to contend with many forms of prejudice in their shops. Sometimes women endured overt sexual harassment; other times they were paid less money or forced to wait longer than other workers for their machines to be repaired. Workers new to these jobs frequently formed alliances with each other to make their work life more bearable.*

### Celia Sapersteen Yanish—machinist—New York City

Before the war I worked in metal shops, assembling locks and doing other assembly work, until 1941 when the government set up defense training schools where they taught you to operate a bench lathe and drill press. There were mostly young men there—I was one of three girls in the school.

When the class was over we were sent to a machine shop. I was very happy. For the first time in my life I was going to be able to do skilled work. We were working on a precise part for the bomb. I didn't know what it was, but I knew that until then only men had done this work.

Most of the men in the shop did not want to go to war. In my department, some even had their eardrums punctured so they wouldn't be drafted. They were afraid we women were taking away their jobs and they resented us. They complained they wouldn't be able to undress in the shop and work half nude like they did before. They said the women would interfere with their work, would distract them.

Not only that, but our foreman was actually a Nazi sympathizer. He was later arrested and released in connection with the discovery of a German U-Boat. So imagine, in come we three girls—and I was Jewish!

I was about 24 at the time and I knew how to handle myself. I didn't laugh at the men's dirty jokes. But another girl who was only 17 did laugh and so the men got more and more brazen. They would be looking up her skirt until she would start to cry.

We worked on a competitive system. You had to keep up

with the man standing next to you because he made more money if he could increase his production. If you slowed down, they would say, "We knew these women would be no damn good." We were exhausted all the time. The men would go home and sit down to a prepared meal, but when the women came home they had to get the meal ready for their family, or themselves if they were single.

It was very rough for a while, but we were determined to stay, and eventually, the majority of the men learned to accept us and respect us as co-workers and union sisters.

Later on, I got another job in a tool and die shop. It was a small place, only about 25 people. I was hired, and after me a young black man. I was the only woman, and he was the only black. We did lathe and drill press work. It was new to both of us. We helped each other—there was nobody else to help us.

There was something special about working with men. They don't take as much crap as girls do, so there's more freedom. On the assembly line in '36, I had to ask for permission to get up. There was an atmosphere of fear, of discipline. Here people walked back and forth and talked freely, and most of the men were friendly. Generally women in the shops weren't given the most skilled jobs, al-

Men and women workers take a break at the Ingalls Shipbuilding Company in Pascagoula, Mississippi. "It was very rough for a while, but we were determined to stay, and eventually the majority of the men learned to accept us and respect us as co-workers and union sisters" (Celia Yanish, machinist). *Official Navy Photograph, National Archives*

Ruth Wolf. *Connie Field*

**"They kept me on an apprentice wage even though I'd been there longer than he had."**

though there was one little woman in the first place I worked who did better than the men, on a tremendous, huge drill press. They even took a promotional picture of her next to that drill press.

I loved that job, because I produced something. I wasn't just putting the screw into the lock. I knew it was precision work, and it required skill. It gave me a self-respect I didn't have before.

Skilled work does wonders for a person's ego. I remember sitting on the subway in New York, going home, and watching black people next to me, who had gotten jobs through the war. They had such an air of dignity about them, of pride in the work they were doing, and I thought, "Why, I must look just the same!"

### Ruth Wolf—foundry worker and furnace operator— Patterson Foundry, Patterson, Ohio, and Crucible Steel Mill, Midland, Pennsylvania

Before the war I worked in the pottery trade. East Liverpool, Ohio, is the pottery center of the world. I worked there from the seventh grade. It's a woman's industry. There were two women to every man. It was a sweat shop affair and the wages were very low.

Shortly after Pearl Harbor had been bombed, I saw an ad in the daily paper which said, "Anyone interested in doing defense work, call or come in to the unemployment office." So I went downtown before work one day, and I signed up. I would work a shift in the pottery shop and then do a session in the training school. They taught us how to run a milling machine and a lathe. After about six weeks' time, they sent me and about twenty other women to report at the Patterson Foundry Company.

I was put on a milling machine, making small pieces for machine guns. It had to be very exact. They told us, "If you don't make these pieces exactly right, it may cost some soldier his life."

Our production quotas were based according to the piece. You had to work exceedingly hard to make the average wage, much less anything over. You were also paid according to the size of the piece, and men always got the bigger pieces which brought more money. One day I turned to this older man, who was working right alongside me. He was very old, and he was handling just the same size pieces I was. I was shocked to find out that he was making much more than I was. Turns out they had kept me on this apprentice wage, even though I'd been there longer than he had. I was spitting mad. Here I was, doing the same work at the same time, and him making more than me!

They had never had women in that foundry before, and both the foremen and the other men there resented us terribly and did all sorts of things against us. We were not allowed to do anything with the machines, only to operate them. If it went bad, we had to call the machinist, who, of course, was a man. And since it was piecework it was very important to get your machine fixed fast. If a man's machine broke down, the machinist would go right away and fix it, but a woman could wait longer than a day.

They timed us so that we could not go to the restroom. At first, we did not even have a restroom—then finally they built one for us. But if the foreman saw you going down those steps more than once or twice in a morning, he'd say, "Why are you leaving that job?"

There was one lady there, Julia, a very big Croatian woman. She worked like a man, and they put her on men's jobs, doing heavy lifting. But they did not pay her as much as they did the men.

One day, she was talking to a union man who was trying to organize the plant. She knew him, and she saw him on this sound truck outside, and so she went over to say hello. The owner of the plant saw her, and they fired her on the spot!

We were all outraged. We said, "No, you will not fire her. She works too hard for you. She is the best worker in the plant. If you fire her, we'll all walk out." And we did! The walkout lasted maybe a day, and then they backed down. But from then on Julia was always a thorn in their side.

I got a taste of that kind of treatment myself, after the union came in. Most of the women there had no experience with unions. But I had been a trustee in the pottery union, so I ended up representing them. That was when the foreman we worked for really started making things rough for me.

I had been working on this milling machine, which I did

very well on. But then one morning, he said, "You go work on that big machine." It was a newer electrical milling machine, which made much bigger pieces. I knew it would be hard for me to handle. I had to stand on a box to reach it.

Linda Martinez operates a press that develops 450 tons of pressure. *International Ness Photo, National Archives*

The girl next to me was a friend, and gave me a few instructions about what to do. She pushed the button to show me something, and then suddenly the machine caught the pieces of the jig and broke them. I wasn't about to say that she had done it, because there was a rule in the shop that no one is to operate another person's machine. She would have lost her job.

The foreman was furious with me, though he could not fire me. Instead, he gave me a five-day suspension. But I knew that many men had broken jigs and that they hadn't done anything to them, so I demanded a release from the company. At that time, the government would not allow you to leave a plant, if you were working on war orders, without a special release.

I had heard that the Crucible Steel mill across the state line, in Midland, Pennsylvania, was thinking of taking women, so I went there once I got my release, and I was in one of the first groups of women they hired. I ran into many of the same things there as in the foundry. Steel, too, had always been a man's industry, and the men were against having us in the plant, even though it was necessary, because so many men were at war. The foreman presented the same problem as the one in the foundry. He couldn't see a woman in there for nothing.

When I hired in, I told them that I knew how to fire an annealing furnace. My husband had taught me years before. I used to bring him his dinner in the furnace room on the nights when he worked overtime, and sometimes I'd stay and keep him company there while he worked. I was interested in what he did, you know, and so he explained to me how it all worked.

I surprised them all at the Crucible mill—they never expected to find a woman who knew how to operate the furnace!

The work I did there was not nearly so hard as in the pottery factory, where you had to lift big loads, and heavy boxes of ware. We used to stand all day long on concrete floors in the pottery factory, which really ruins your feet. In the steel mill, we did not have anything like that. It was easy work, more intelligent work. You weren't just standing up all day and working like a robot. □

*Full employment during peacetime was proposed in Congress as early as 1944. The Kilgore-Murray Bill to broaden employment and retraining benefits for laid-off workers and veterans and to finance industrial reconversion was defeated in the Senate. When similar legislation (S.B. 380) came before the Senate in 1945, the following debate over the possibility of full employment in peacetime took place between Senator William Fulbright (Dem., Arkansas), Senator James E. Murray (Dem., Montana), and Secretary of the Treasury Frederick M. Vinson.*

## "Full employment? It is inconsistent with the system of private enterprise."

*Fulbright:* Do you consider in the operation of our system of private enterprise that a certain number, and I would not begin to try to set the number—but that a certain number of unemployed is an essential part of that system in order to allow for the flexibility of new businesses? In other words, if we assume an absolute full employment you couldn't start any new businesses, could you?

*Vinson:* Well, the question of full employment and the numbers involved of course—the goal is the nearest to it you can come. Of course, you never can have any absolute. And as you point out, it might not be a happy thing to have it absolute.

*Fulbright:* It is really inconsistent with the system of private enterprise.

*Vinson:* My notion about that is that I will worry about it if and when we get to it.

*Fulbright:* My thought was this, if that is true, just assuming for illustration the number was a million or whatever, it may be then that a million of unemployed at any one time should be considered as part of the cost of industry and provision should be made to sustain that particular incident in our system, shouldn't it? Isn't that what is at the basis of social security, the idea that that is part of the cost?

*Vinson:* If they are eligible for social security benefits, of course, they would get them.

*Fulbright:* And, of course, the fact they are here and available for work is an essential attribute of the private enterprise system as opposed to the State system?

*Vinson:* Yes, there is bound to be a considerable number of unemployed and unemployable.

*Fulbright:* And there ought to be, in order to have this system work.

*Senator Murray:* Mr. Secretary, if this bill had been in effect during the 1920's, would it not have been effective in preventing many of the conditions that developed that brought us to the crash of 1929?

*Vinson:* Well, it is my thought, Senator, that if it had been on the books and the program had been worked up and all, and when it was seen what either had happened or was going to happen, that it would have helped very much if taken hold of early enough and might have prevented it without great cost.

*Murray:* For instance, in that period the trend toward monopoly and undue concentration of business was going forward at a very rapid pace, and we also had high tariffs, and during that period the farm income was falling down, farmers were becoming bankrupt around the country. All of these matters could have been examined into as a result of the provisions of this bill, and many things could have been done to have prevented what happened.

*Chairman:* Are there any questions? (There was no response.) □

Congressional Record, 1945

"When you're unemployed, the days stretch out. Each hour is the same" (Grace Lee Boggs, electrical worker).
*Dorothea Lange Collection, Oakland Museum*

# WOMEN JOIN THE UNIONS

*I had wanted to work in some big aircraft plant, like we were beginning to see in the movies. But Kaufsky's shop— well, it was an old dive. We were very good producers, but we were earning far less than the men who were doing the same work. Blanche and I went down to United Electrical Workers Union; we started wearing union buttons, and Mr. Kaufsky's face changed. He didn't like us anymore. We were no longer his girls.*

—Lola Weixel, welder, New York

Women's membership in unions grew four-fold during World War II. This represented an enormous jump but not the first time that women had ever joined unions. In the 1840's, women formed labor organizations in the textile industries of New England, and the 1860's witnessed the beginnings of organizations such as the all-women's Collar Laundry Workers of Troy, New York, and the shoe factory workers of the national Daughters of St. Crispin. Nevertheless, because of the persistent sexual divisions of labor in all industries which developed in the U.S. in the late nineteenth century, many other strong unions remained all-male in membership. Although the National Labor Union and the Knights of Labor in the 1870's encouraged women's participation on a national level, local practice frequently contradicted official policies.

The American Federation of Labor (AFL), founded in 1886, grew to become the most stable of the national labor organizations, and by 1904, it represented two million American workers, 80 percent of the nation's union members. Organizing skilled workers along craft lines, the AFL allowed member unions such as the Molders or the Boot and Shoe Workers to establish exclusionary policies towards women workers in their trades. Male-identified crafts thus remained the domain of men, and women entered the AFL only when they were working in "women's occupations" such as in the garment industry or as cigar rollers. Prejudice against women's competency or suitability for the trades was also reflected in the beliefs of turn-of-the-century AFL officials like its president, Samuel Gompers, who stated that women could become "unsexed" by joining unions.

In the late 1930's, the Congress of Industrial Organizations (CIO) began organizing manufacturing industries hitherto largely ignored by the AFL. As a result, millions of workers in auto, electrical, rubber, metal, clothing, mining and textile companies entered new CIO unions. Women contributed significantly to CIO organizing drives, particularly in employ-

(Facing Page)   Women's numbers in the unionized workforce, including the West Coast Kaiser Shipyards, quadrupled during the war. *Kaiser Industries*

ment areas traditionally considered within women's "proper sphere"—hotel and restaurant services, the needle trades, clerical work, cigar rolling, and retail clerking.

Militant women also helped win major strikes within mostly male industries. In 1937, during one of the most decisive labor battles of the decade, the Women's Emergency Brigade courageously fought street skirmishes to help the United Auto Workers secure its first contract with General Motors in the long sit-down strike in Flint, Michigan.

Because the CIO movement sought to organize *every* worker in a plant, whether skilled

Workers successfully picketed for union recognition at Henry Ford's River Rouge Plant near Dearborn, Michigan, in 1941. *Archives of Labor and Urban Affairs, Wayne State University*

Picketers support the UAW-CIO sit-down strike at Dodge Main in Hamtramck, Michigan, in 1937. *Archives of Labor and Urban Affairs, Wayne State University*

or unskilled by AFL definition, the CIO extended a broader, more democratic vision of the rights of all industrial workers. The CIO's success in conducting militant sit-down strikes in the late 1930s, the financial support and picket-line respect given these strikes by workers in other CIO industries, and the communication between unions at conventions and among workers through educational pamphlets and leaflets made this organized labor movement a decisive force in the American economy.

Although the number of women workers in the economy has almost doubled since World War II and over 50 percent of all adult women work outside the home today, only one woman worker in six belongs to a union. Overall there has been a slight decline in the percentage of unionized workers in the labor force—from 35 percent in 1950 to 21 percent in 1980—in part a measure of the strength of the anti-union Taft-Hartley Act and a growing anti-union climate. Passed in 1947, the Taft-Hartley law seriously affects the labor movement's ability to organize new unions, especially with its "right-to-work" clause limiting the union shop, secondary boycott restrictions, and sanctioning of government injunctions to halt strikes.

## World War II Changes the Labor Movement

With the outbreak of World War II and the need to fight fascism with troops and weapons, both the industrial unions of the CIO and the trades and crafts unions of the AFL made agreements with the government not to strike until the war was won. In exchange for this pledge of "no strikes," the unions won from management and government a "maintenance of membership" agreement which promised that the unions could continue to function in plants where they already existed after they converted to producing war goods.

Union leadership also cooperated with the government through the duration of the war. During World War I, the AFL President Samuel Gompers had been brought onto the War Labor Board. At the beginning of World War II, President Franklin Roosevelt appointed CIO Amalgamated Clothing Workers leader Sidney Hillman to his National Defense Advisory Committee with the barely veiled warning, "Sidney, I expect you to keep labor in step." As a result of this labor-government cooperation, wages in most industries were controlled throughout the war. Prices were supposed to be controlled too, but they rose, nevertheless. In addition, union officials were prohibited from endorsing work stoppages and, in fact, were obligated by the War Labor Board to bring workers back into the shop. As former munitions worker Margaret Wright remembers the era, "You know, if you even talked about union activities too much, you were kind of unpatriotic."

Despite these efforts to force unions to relinquish their independence, workers with grievances held unsanctioned wildcat strikes throughout the war years. Although the strikes were short-lived and local, there were more of them during World War II than during the entire strife-torn 1930's. A major breach of the no-strike pledge came in the summer of 1943 when the United Mine Workers walked out over their wages, which were not keeping up with inflation.

While wage increases proved difficult to negotiate, fringe benefits became a more important aspect of union bargaining. Under the cost-plus defense contract system, negotiations for health and medical insurance, pensions, and holiday and vacation pay were more likely to result favorably for the union, because companies could pass the costs of these benefits on to the government.

Although union membership grew rapidly during the war, rank and file union members found themselves more distanced from their leaders than during the previous decade. Leaders had to keep up with numerous contract violations; thus they had little opportunity to educate members about their rights and responsibilities. The establishment of dues check-off, or automatic payroll deductions of union dues, further eroded communication between leaders and workers who had previously traded information at least once a month when paying dues. Attendance at union meetings also dropped because of the mandatory overtime in most war plants.

Union leaders' participation in government policy-making councils helped insure that union gains made in the 1930's would be maintained in the 1940's, but the presence of business representatives on these same boards also meant that some decisions made by these councils did not reflect the wishes of workers on the shop floor. Nevertheless, decent wages were continued in union shops throughout the war, whether workers were male or female.

## Unions Hold the Line

Women who entered union shops or who helped organize unions during the war were impressed with the differences in wages and working conditions that union membership meant. Lola Weixel remembers that a union contract in her welding shop brought an 80 percent wage increase for everyone, including the equalization of wages for black women who until then had been working for five cents less an hour. Similarly, Margaret Wright recalls the power she gained as a union member:

If they asked me to work overtime, I got paid for overtime, so it was a big difference there. It was more like I had control over what was going on. If things didn't work right, I could always go to the union. Who could I go to doing domestic work? There was no union there. I either had to quit, pack and leave, or whatever. But I did have some say-so at a job in the factory.

Women workers also had many instances of positive union intervention when trouble erupted at work. Wanita Allen remembers how a black union steward confronted an issue of racial discrimination among workers when white women refused to work with black women at Ford's River Rouge plant. Similarly, after Margaret Wright was fired for a quarrel with a white worker, her union representative had her reinstated in five minutes. She remembered thinking, "My God, I've got justice for once."

Women's membership in unions grew from 800,000 in 1939 to more than 3 million in 1945. Some of this growth stemmed from active union organizing. The primary reason, however, was the "maintenance of membership" policy, which meant that when a woman entered a plant, she became automatically a union member. However, women union members rarely attained local or international leadership positions, and when they did become officials and leaders it was only in industries which were traditionally considered in the women's sphere, for example, among the electrical and needle trades unions. In most cases, unions continued to be directed and staffed entirely by men.

As union leaders addressed their priority issues like wages, health and safety, and speed-ups, other problems that specifically concerned many women war workers were put aside. Foundry worker Wanita Allen, for instance,

The Women's Department of the United Auto Workers was established in 1944, when women's membership in the International had risen to 28 percent. After the war, the Women's Department continued to educate union sisters who survived the massive layoffs and to lobby with other working women's groups for legislation guaranteeing equal pay. *Archives of Labor and Urban Affairs, Wayne State University*

considered approaching the union because most of the women assigned to work in the blast furnace "hell hole" were black, but she soon realized that she "better keep still for a while," because it had been so hard for her to get her job in the first place. Union leaders also allowed her repeated written grievances over forced overtime to pile up. "I was trying so hard to make them see that ten hours was just too much for me. I didn't mind eight and an occasional nine, but ten was just too much."

A major stumbling block to full participation by women in union activities was the pressure created by women's double day. While some men complained that women were not active in local union affairs, union meetings often were

scheduled at late hours that interfered with most women's second job at home as mothers and wives, housekeepers and cooks. As Lola Weixel recalls, women would mainly talk among themselves about the problems created by the "double day." When she did broach the topic with a sympathetic union organizer, it was simply, " 'Oh well, that's life.' They didn't know how it felt."

More than merely being unsympathetic, several unions in fact outspokenly opposed bringing new female and minority male workers into their "brotherhoods." In many defense plants, separate seniority lists, as well as separate job classifications, were maintained for women and black men throughout the war, a discriminatory practice permitted by most international unions.

Union contracts too, often contained clauses which limited women's stay for the duration only, or limited women's seniority and gave job retention priority to men when layoffs were scheduled. The policy of paying women equal (or almost equal) wages was supported largely in order to preserve a high wage scale for returning veterans. This assumption was reiterated by a UAW official addressing women at a CIO convention in 1943 when he urged, "It is your job to maintain the unions and to see that the men have good conditions to come back to."

Some unions, however, did take steps to accommodate the heavy demands of work and family on women war workers. The United Electrical Workers, whose female membership was 40 percent by 1945, urged stores in industrial communities to stay open longer hours so that women could shop for food and other necessities. They also paid some notice to the need for child care. Similarly, in the UAW, which was 28 percent female by the end of the war, women succeeded in forming a Women's Bureau in the International organization. Its purpose was to educate new women workers about their rights and responsibilities under

Women laid off in 1945 at the Ford plant in Highland Park, Michigan, fight back against the company's discrimination. *National Archives*

New wartime workers line up at the Rubber Workers' Union in Buffalo, New York, in 1943. Many women were not protected by the unions after the war, and women were laid off at a rate 75% higher than men.
*Library of Congress*

the contract and to help protect these rights.

In 1944 this UAW Women's Bureau extended its mandate by establishing model clauses in union contracts barring discrimination based on sex or marital status, and setting forth non-discriminatory seniority and promotional systems and adequate work breaks for all employees. Joining with other unions and women's groups, it lobbied to introduce the Pepper-Morse bill into Congress in 1945, a bill which would have prohibited paying different wages for equal work. It would also have prohibited bypassing women's seniority, except for the super seniority accorded returning veterans. The bill failed to win approval then, and it was reintroduced in various forms in the years that followed. Finally, in 1963, the Federal Equal Pay Act became law.

### When the War Ended

Although unions accepted women into their ranks with some enthusiasm and support during the war, after the armistice the unions only half-heartedly challenged management's decision to dismiss women war workers. In the absence of adequate government planning for reconversion of military production to peacetime manufacturing, a massive unemployment crisis occurred directly after the war. Women war workers, laid off at a rate 75 percent higher than men, bore the brunt of post-war economic dislocation.

There were some important instances where women successfully pressured their unions for non-discriminatory layoffs. In the electrical and clothing industries, women continued to be employed at decent wages. At Dodge Main in Detroit and a few other plants, women won their battle to stay on. At Inland Steel in Gary, Indiana, women were kept on but "bumped down" from the steel mills and hearths to the labor pool and the tin mill, areas in the steel industry which were considered women's work. As Lola Weixel sadly remembers, "We were no longer comrades in arms. We were competitors for what little there was. There was a lot of money around but it wasn't in our pockets." □

## WOMEN'S STATUS IN UNIONS DURING THE WAR

| Union | Industry | % of Women & Status | Women in Leadership | Special Services | Childcare | Seniority & Equal-Pay Issue | Post-War Layoffs | Notes |
|---|---|---|---|---|---|---|---|---|
| **United Electrical Workers (UE-CIO)** | Electrical; munitions; aircraft and motor vehicle parts; some machine shops. | 1945: 40%. Women full members. | Many activists and organizers; many local leaders; a few significant leaders in International. | Encouraged community stores to keep late hours for workers' convenience. | Campaigned for federal funds for child care. | Took cases to War Labor Board when violations came up. The contract policy of equal pay for equal work was to maintain post-war wage standards for men. | International policy support-ed equal sen-iority rights, but at local level separate sen-iority lists were kept and enforcement varied. Other devices were used in some locals, e.g., in all GM plants, seniority was within occupa-tional grouping. Some locals fought to pre-serve women's seniority rights. | UE organize some all-wo plants, e.g., s electrical ass bly plants. So other shops all male. Poli on women va Locals often odds with International |
| **United Auto Workers (UAW-CIO)** | Aircraft; tanks & jeeps; motor vehicle parts; munitions; some machine shops. | 1945: 28%. Women full members. | Some local leadership. Women's Com-mittee in locals. International leadership all male except for Women's Bureau (est. 1944). | Women's Bureau wrote model contract clauses. Union counseling for out-of-plant problems: health, child-care, housing, transportation. | Campaigned for federal funds for childcare. | The contract policy of equal pay for equal work was to maintain post-war wage stan-dards for men. | | Locals had autonomy in termining an enforcing con tract. Freque deviations fro International policy. |
| **United Steelworkers of America (USWA-CIO)** | Steel milling; steel process-ing; some munitions. | 1945: 11%. Women full members. | No women in International leadership. | None. | Neither union nor companies made efforts towards childcare. | | Contracts were written for the duration only. Therefore, women had no rights to post-war employment. | A "top-down" organization. Locals had v little autonom International Districts still resist women organizing within locals. |
| **International Brotherhood of Boiler-makers and Shipfitters (Boilermakers AFL)** | Machine shops; shipbuilding. | 1944: 9.5%. All women were assigned to temporary trainee status. Black women assigned to black auxiliaries. | No women in leadership. | None. | Companies (e.g., Kaiser) provided child care. Union not involved. | | As trainees for the dura-tion, women had no rights to post-war employment. | No activity at local level in shipyards. Du collected but meetings. Se arate auxiliar for blacks. |
| **International Association of Machinists (IAM-AFL)** | Machine shops and aircraft; some munitions. | Union kept no records. | No women in International leadership; some women stewards in local lodges. | None. | No union efforts for child care. | | Straight seniority with emergency lay-off plan for immediate post-war era. | Concentrate on West Coa (Los Angeles |

Lola Weixel in the 1940's.

# "We were no longer 'his girls'."

*Lola Weixel describes how she first learned about unions and helped organize her small shop in New York City. She also reflects on the pressures of women's double day which some unions were more responsive to than others.*

### Lola Weixel—welder
### Kaufsky's Welding Shop, New York City

I knew about unions from the time I was a little girl, because my cousins were garment workers, and they always sang union songs to me. I read the union literature from the International Ladies Garment Worker Union, the stories of organizing the shops. And I had met women who said that they had been shot at running across roofs. My cousin was brought into the house after having been terribly assaulted by the police when I was about seven, because of being involved in organizing efforts. I took unionism in with my mother's milk, so to speak. So it wasn't so unusual for me to be involved when I went to work myself in shops during the war.

At Kaufsky's we were paid very little. We worked all day for 30 cents an hour. We had no rest periods, or anything of the sort. Of the nine women that I was hired with, none of us came from a family that could take care of us, and we always talked about the fact that we weren't earning a living. We certainly wanted to help with the war effort—all of us were involved in those feelings. But still, we had to earn a living, and we were not doing so.

When we found out that the men were earning more than we were, Blanche and I went down to the office of the United Electrical Workers Union, which was a very good union. We told our story, and they were very interested. We were newsworthy, I guess, and also it was a way in for them. They assigned a very good organizer to us. She came down to the shop, spoke to the people during lunch hour, on the street. And of course we did too.

We started to wear union buttons, and Mr. Kaufsky's face changed, he didn't like us anymore. We were no longer "his girls!" And he had a foreman, Emil, who felt personally insulted by our union buttons. 'Cause he said that he was good to us—and he *was* good to us—that had nothing to do with it. Anyway, it took us a few weeks. We got union cards signed.

Then, one morning, we came to work, and the door was locked. We couldn't come in—we were locked out. So, Thelma, our union organizer, called the newspapers. They came with their cameras, and they took pictures of us, and wrote a story.

Then the union filed a complaint with the National Labor

Women union officials at General Aircraft in Long Island City, New York, prepare for a negotiating session in 1943. *Archives of Labor and Urban Affairs, Wayne State University*

Relations Board [NLRB] saying that we wanted to work, but that we were being harassed and locked out. We really did want to work for the war effort, and Mr. Kaufsky wouldn't permit us to. His attitude had changed since the union, and of course now he said we were no good, we were unskilled, we didn't know what we were doing. He said that we were only good for being married and having babies. That's all we were good for.

Well, the NLRB ruled in our favor, so we became members of the Electrical Workers Union. And the change in our money was fantastic—it was about an 80 percent raise. The union contract brought us almost up to par with the men. We also had some black women workers in the shop. They had never before told us, but only when we were organizing the union did we find out that they were paid five cents less per hour than the white women workers. Talk about cheap!

When we started organizing at Kaufsky's it was easy to win the women over to the idea of the union. But with the men it was different. They were frightened. They had been with Kaufsky a long time, and it had never occurred to them. Plus they were getting a better deal than we were, so they weren't so enthusiastic. But when we were through, we were really in with the union. Kaufsky's was going to be a union shop for ever and ever.

The period of organizing is always a difficult time for workers, because you're exposed. You wear union buttons. And you come up against attitudes of other workers that are sometimes surprising. You might be good friends with someone, and then you find out that this person doesn't really believe in unions. The boss certainly doesn't, and so you're subjected to a great deal of harassment.

Later, when I went to work at General Aircraft, I was also part of an organizing drive there. The plant was right next to the Steinway piano complex, and so the Furniture Workers Union was interested in organizing us. We did a lot of woodwork on the gliders we were making, so that seemed okay.

But, there was the difficulty of union meetings taking place late at night, and after a long work day. The UE was different, but the Furniture Workers Union people did not seem to understand that the life of a woman at home is different than that of a man. So there was always this antagonism between the women and the union leaders. I knew I felt it very strongly. I was living with my husband's mother at the time, and various other relatives—we had all doubled up together for the war, and there were lots of things to be done. We were a large family so there were lots of dishes every night, pots to clean. My mother-in-law was not young, and I would certainly not see her do the dishes. So I felt the need to pitch in, and then I had to take care of my laundry besides. We also had a baby in the house, so all of us women would be busy washing diapers. You know, we didn't have the sort of things you have now. There was a lot of work to be done in a household and it was done by the women, period. Now my brother-in-law also lived there—he worked at the Brooklyn Navy Yard, and I guess I just accepted it, 'cause after dinner he would just lie down on the couch and listen to jazz records.

Anyway, this made it hard for women to get out to union meetings, but it was something that could not be explained to the men. We'd discuss it informally sometimes. Like I used to ride home with one of the organizers in the Furniture Workers, he lived near me, and I would mention it going home in the car. He'd say, "Oh, what are you com-

Two shipyard workers, perhaps a husband and wife, compare paychecks in Richmond, California. Although women earned higher wages than ever before, they did not necessarily receive as much pay as men. *Dorothea Lange Collection, Oakland Museum*

plaining about, you're young!" You know, that sort of thing. It was never taken very seriously. There was just no understanding or respect given to women for their life outside the workplace, and I admit, I myself never really gave much thought to women workers who had children—how were they managing? But I certainly knew where I hurt, and that was that I had little sleep and had to be at work very early in the morning, and work a long day at a hard job. I was always at loggerheads with the union men over this. It was a joke to them—you know, "Oh well, the women . . . ." The men had wives at home running their houses for them, they just didn't know how it felt.

At the union meetings, we discussed issues of the shop. We discussed the forthcoming elections, and how the signing up was going in various departments. Things like that. I don't recall the question of late meetings, or the problems of women coming up at the meetings at all. Women would talk among ourselves about it, though there were some women who didn't see it as very important either.

The Furniture Workers did not take up issues that are today called "women's issues." Problems of day care, or of equal pay. We had job classifications, and your pay depended on where you worked and how long you'd been there. There were certainly areas where women did not work, however, and that used to make me very angry.

When I compare the Furniture Workers Union with the Electrical Workers, I would say that the UE came closer to the worker—certainly to the women worker. They were always available to us. They were interested in our problems. We had a wonderful organizer, Thelma, who compared very favorably with the one from the Furniture Workers. But it was a good union, too. It was an honest and straightforward union, though I don't think they were as advanced,in terms of helping a worker with life, as the UE was. But certainly, we were better off with a union with problems than without a union. At least there was something you could deal with. If the boss didn't treat you right, there was someone to speak for you. I guess some people can make deals with the boss to get what they need, but in the end, an individual has very little power, a very small voice.  □

# Union Songs and War Songs

*Songs are an important cultural heritage of the American labor movement. At the turn of the century, the Industrial Workers of the World (IWW) used them with great success in organizing campaigns. CIO campaign songs likewise reflect the irreverent and tough union spirit of the 1930's and 1940's. Woody Guthrie's "You've Got to Go Down" is a recruiting song, much like the missionary ballad from which it takes its melody. Written and sung during the early '40s, it carries on the CIO organizing spirit of solidarity and commitment. With a different message, the song "UAW CIO" is an expression of workers' pride in producing goods for the war effort. It also reveals organized labor's strong identification with government interests during the war.*

1. You've got to go down and join the union —
   You've got to join it for yourself.
   There ain't nobody going to join it for you —
   You've got to to go down and join the union for yourself.

2. Sister's got to go down and join the union —
   She's got to join it for herself.
   There ain't nobody going to join it for her —
   She's got to go down and join the union for herself.

3. Brother's got to go down and join the union —
   He's got to join it for himself.
   There ain't nobody going to join it for him —
   He's got to go down and join the union for himself.

4. Everybody's going down to join the union —
   They've got to join it for themselves.
   There ain't nobody going to join it for them —
   They've got to go down and join the union for themselves.

Women in unions made close friendships with co-workers who shared hard work, financial independence and a sense of accomplishment. *National Archives*

# YOU'VE GOT TO GO DOWN

Words and music by
WOODY GUTHRIE

*With steady beat*

You've got to go down _____ and join the u - nion,

You've got to join _____ it for your - self.

There ain't no - bo - dy _____ going to join it for you,

You've got to go down and join the u - nion for your - self. _____

# U. A. W.- C. I. O.

Words and music by
BESS AND BALDWIN HAWES

I was stan-ding round a de-fense town one day When I thought I o-ver-heard a sol-dier say: "E-v'ry tank in our camp has that U - A-dou-ble-U stamp, And I'm U - A-dou-ble-U too, I'm proud to say." It's the U - A dou-ble U - C - I - O, makes the ar-my roll and go;

Turning out the jeeps and tanks and airplanes ev'ry day. It's the
U-A-double U-C-I-O, makes the army roll and go, Puts wheels on the U. S. A.

2. I was there when the union came to town;
   I was there when old Henry Ford went down;
   I was standing by Gate Four when I heard the people roar,
   "They ain't gonna kick the autoworkers around."

3. I was there on that cold December day
   When we heard about Pearl Harbor far away;
   I was down in Cadillac Square when the union rallied there
   To put those plans for pleasure cars away.

4. There'll be a union label in Berlin
   When those union boys in uniform march in;
   And rolling in the ranks there'll be UAW tanks:
   Roll Hitler out and roll the union in.

# BLACK WORKERS FIGHT FOR DOUBLE VICTORY

*When we first got into the war, the country wasn't pre-*
*pared. And as the manpower in the country was getting*
*pulled into the service, all of the industries were wide open.*
*So they decided, "Well, we better let some of those blacks*
*come in." Then after the source of men dried up, they began*
*to let women come in. The doors were opened.*
　　　　　　　　　　—Lyn Childs, shipburner, San Francisco

During World War II the employment status of black women and men went through a remarkable transformation. War employment in industrial centers accelerated the migration of blacks to western and northern cities, where industries paid much higher wages than in the South. By 1945, segregation in the military had been significantly challenged, and while institutional racism was far from dead, many of its legal and governmental supports were gone.

But by no means did these changes come easily. Most black troops in World War II, in fact, were drafted into segregated units under the command of white officers to serve as messmen or "maids to the braid." In the Navy, official segregation ended only after black-white riots, black hunger strikes, and finally the court martial of 50 black sailors who refused to load ammunition ships in California after an explosion killed 342 men, a majority of whom were black. In 1948 President Harry Truman ordered the complete integration of all the armed forces.

Because the struggle against racism by black workers was highly organized during the war, changes in their economic and social status were broad and dramatic. But other minority groups were also deeply affected by the sudden shifts in production demands and political policy. Mexican-American men were drafted into both black and white military units, but the number of Mexican-American women who entered defense industries was small. Some midwestern steel plants employed Mexican-American women in production, but on the West Coast they continued to work on farms and in canneries at low wages, often replacing the Japanese agricultural workers who after Pearl Harbor were evacuated by the trainload to internment camps.

Government propaganda films and posters recruiting war workers for factories were aimed only at white people. Even when more workers were badly needed in factories, many companies refused to hire blacks. Not infrequently blacks could be seen carrying picket

(Facing Page)　These two new welders found work at the Landers, Ferry, and Clark plant in New Britain, Connecticut. *Gordon Parks, Library of Congress*

As war production geared up in industrial cities, blacks were not hired for newly opened jobs. Vigorous organizing brought about Executive Order 8802 which established the Fair Employment Practices Commission. *Schomburg Center Collection, New York Public Library*

Families migrated around the country throughout the thirties in search of agricultural work. In the forties, defense production drew 2 million families out of the South to the North and West. *Jack Delano, Library of Congress.*

signs reading, "Hitler must own this plant, Ne-groes can't work here" and "If we must fight, why can't we work?"

Most blacks did not believe that the war would miraculously end America's legacy of racial discrimination. The blows that were struck to Jim Crow, as racial discrimination was called, came from a combination of economic necessity to hire more workers and militant struggle by blacks to gain jobs and a measure of equality. In mid-1941, for example, American involvement in the growing European conflict stimulated industrial production. A. Phillip Randolph, who was then leader of the Brother-hood of Sleeping Car Porters, the AFL's first all-black union, met together with other black leaders and called for mass public demonstra-tions by black people and organizations in Washington, D.C., to win a place in war work. The call to march, which was printed in many black community newspapers and posted in many churches read:

> The Negro's stake in national defense is big. It consists of jobs, thousands of jobs. It may rep-resent millions, yes, hundreds of millions of dollars in wages. It consists of new industrial opportunities and hope. This is worth fighting for.

The threat of 100,000 militant blacks de-scending on the capital under the banner, "We loyal American citizens demand the right to work and fight for our country," pressured President Franklin Roosevelt to issue Executive Order 8802 just in time to forestall the march. This groundbreaking order established the Fair Employment Practices Commission (FEPC) which outlawed discrimination in the defense industries because of race, creed, color or national origin. As black munitions worker Margaret Wright remembered, it was only Randolph's threats of marching on Washing-ton, D.C., that "made Roosevelt give this proc-lamation, because no one does anything—you never get anything—out of the goodness of people's hearts."

While some blacks optimistically viewed Ex-ecutive Order 8802 as the most important po-litical and economic step for them since post–Civil War legislation, the order's jurisdiction extended only to defense plants, and even there it was not consistently enforced. Many other black activists continued to push for a law that would prevent discrimination in hiring practices and withhold rights granted by the National Labor Relations Act—including the right to vote for a union of choice and the outlawing of certain unfair employer practices —to unions which denied blacks full member-ship. But it was not until the Civil Rights Act of 1964 that federal legislation prohibiting racial discrimination came into being.

### Jim Crow Maintains Itself During the War Years

Companies continued to discriminate against blacks throughout the war, and government moved to counter this discrimination only when it was forced to by black activists. Many unions perpetuated these Jim Crow practices by excluding blacks altogether or giving them second-class status at best. Fair Employment Practices Commission hearings in 1943 and 1944 exposed the discriminatory policies of the Boilermakers' union which required black workers to pay high initiation fees and dues to join segregated "auxiliary locals" which rarely or never met, were unrecognized in other in-dustries, and gave them no rights in the regular union. When in 1944 Marinship Company in Sausalito, California, fired 1,700 black work-ers who refused to pay dues unless they could join the regular Boilermakers' local, it took

Training schools like Bethune-Coleman College in Daytona Beach, Florida, offered short-term courses to prepare black women for jobs. Black women's wages, on the average, rose 1000 percent. *Gordon Parks, Library of Congress*

Within black communities, active local organizations supported defense plant workers. When some Detroit clergymen heard about job openings, they would use their influence to get men—and later women—into the plants by writing recommendations. "Double Victory" clubs (meaning victory abroad over fascism *and* victory at home over racial discrimination) would meet on weekends to encourage blacks to stand up for their rights at the workplace and in the community.

> We talked about our rights and how we needed to stick together to get a greater degree of recognition in the plant in terms of being sure that you got upgraded when you're supposed to. It was there that I got the strength and the courage to really get involved with the union.
> —Lillian Hatcher, riveter and early staff member of the UAW Women's Bureau

Community groups also worked to desegregate restaurants near the plants, and there was always an informal "grapevine" which kept people alerted to what was happening in each plant from shift to shift.

When crises erupted, unofficial strikes occurred, despite the wartime no-strike pledge made by the unions. The summer of 1943, for example, saw several work stoppages by black workers in St. Louis, Missouri, to protest working conditions as well as the refusal of a company to promote black workers to higher job levels.

Racial tensions among workers were often resolved by direct action. When black shipyard burner Lyn Childs raised her cutting torch and threatened a white foreman who was abusing a Filipino worker, she knew that her job was at stake. But her fellow workers' recognition that she was defending the rights of all of them, black and white, made a crucial difference. As she remembers,

many months of expensive legislation before the California Supreme Court ordered them reinstated. By then the war was over.

Throughout the war, black workers continued to address the issue of equal treatment on the job and within the unions and to use the FEPC as an appeal board for obvious cases of discrimination. The fight against discrimination in the Boilermakers' was finally won in 1946. The Urban League and the National Association for the Advancement of Colored People proved instrumental in developing these cases.

I turned my torch off and the intercom aboard ship started to announce, "Lyn Childs, report to Colonel Hickman immediately." So I said, "I guess this is it," and I went into his office. And behind me came all of these men. I said, "Where are you guys going?" They said, "We're going with you." Hickman says, "I just wanted to see Lyn Childs," and they said, "Well you see all of us because we're all down there, and we didn't have guts enough to do what she did, and we're with her." He said, "Well, never mind what I called you for. Go back to work." Well, going with all these people taught me one thing. That when a bunch of people come with you, that could make a

colonel say, "Hush! Get out of here, go back to work."

While racial discrimination survived the war years within many industries and unions as well as in the military service, blacks nevertheless made substantial economic and social gains. Between 1940 and 1944, the percentage of black women in industry rose from 6.5 percent to 18 percent of the workforce, and their wages rose as much as 1000 per cent over pre-war work. The number of black skilled workers doubled in those same years, as did the number of blacks holding federal government jobs. The

In February 1945, 100 members of the Shipyard Workers' Committee Against Discrimination marched in pouring rain to the Boilermakers Union Hall at 11th and Clay in Oakland to protest their exclusion from the union. Membership in the black "auxiliary" cost $15 more than in the union, and cards read "Cooks, Waiters and Janitors Association." *Ray Thompson Collection, Berkeley*

wages of black families increased from 40 percent to 60 percent of white families' wages, and by 1945, there were 1¼ million black union members, some six times more than in 1940.

Moving mainly from service, domestic, and agricultural work, black workers felt liberated by this change in breadwinning power, social status, and dignity.

> We'd never had any opportunity to do that kind of work. Do you think that if you did domestic work all of your life, where you'd cleaned somebody's toilets and did all the cooking for some lazy characters who were sitting on top, and you finally got a chance where you can get a dignified job, you wouldn't fly through the door?
>
> —Lyn Childs, shipburner

### Moving and Making New Communities

But being able to get these new defense industry jobs often meant moving to where the jobs were. As a result, over 2 million Americans, many of them blacks, were uprooted from family, friends, and neighborhoods when they moved West and to northern industrial cities. As more people settled into old towns and cities, existing housing facilities and community services were pushed beyond their capacity. Many families were forced to double-up in shacks or hastily thrown-up quonset huts and military-like barracks. Instant new neighborhoods were formed under these strange circumstances. After Executive Order 9066 forced Japanese Americans into internment camps, blacks poured into newly available housing in San Francisco's Fillmore district where they continue to live today.

Tensions over housing and services occasionally erupted into violent confrontations between whites and blacks. In 1940–1941, there were neighborhood race riots in Dallas. In the summer of 1943, riots over jobs in Mobile, Alabama, and Beaumont, Texas, and racial flare-ups over police brutality against blacks in New York's Harlem left those communities burned and bleeding. At the Sojourner Truth housing project in Detroit in 1942, street fighting broke out between blacks and whites, but city-wide riots were averted through active organizing by blacks and the city's CIO unions, who successfully kept the conflict localized. Nevertheless, the following summer brought violence to Detroit; at least 34 people were killed in the black community where the memory of "Bloody Monday" on Belle Isle lingers on today.

### Victory! For Whom?

The dream that the war would bring permanent economic improvement for black workers ended even before the troops were home. Blacks, like women, were last hired and thus first fired. The vast majority had not been allowed to move into skilled job classifications. When orders in shipbuilding, aircraft, munitions, and explosives factories declined, unemployment soared, and black workers were affected at a rate 2½ times greater than white workers. With the cancellation of the FEPC in 1946, the federal government ended its aggressive commitment to employment of blacks on equal terms with whites. Nevertheless, Margaret Wright remembers clearly how the war changed black people's expectations:

> A lot of blacks that were share cropping, doing menial work and stuff, got into the army and saw how other things were and how things could be. They decided they did not want to go back to what they were doing before. They did not want to walk behind a plow, they wouldn't get on the back of the bus anymore.

An era had ended, but these changes helped spark the civil rights struggles of the fifties and sixties. □

Precious Mack. *Connie Field*

# "We had 12 people in that one-room trailer."

*Welder Precious Mack and foundry worker Wanita Allen experienced overt racial discrimination in many forms during the war. When Precious Mack moved to California, she found that black migrants seeking housing in the "promised land" were not much better off than in the Jim Crow South. Wanita Allen's effort to break the color bar at the Murray Auto Body plant in Detroit, on the other hand, shows how black union activists could occasionally make Executive Order 8802 (which established the Fair Employment Practices Commission) more than a paper victory.*

## Precious Mack — welder
### Kaiser Shipyard, Richmond, California

I had read about California in my geography books, and seen all the lemon trees. I thought it was out of this world. I never even dreamed that someday we'd get to the promised land. But my uncle Jimmy came out here in '39, and he kept on insisting that my daddy come too. It was hard to get Daddy to leave the South, but finally he did in 1942. We came out first, and then he got enough money to send for mother and the rest.

We came to Richmond where Uncle Jimmy was working in the shipyards. We took the bus. I don't remember how many days it took us. Boy! It was hell. We had to stand for so many miles, the bus was so crowded. There were soldiers riding with us, and all kinds of people—babies, and women with children. The kids would sleep on the floor of the bus. We had to just step over each other. It was like a moving pig pen.

The bus was segregated until we got to some part of Texas. There were empty seats in the front one time, but we didn't dare sit up there, 'cause we were raised in the South, and we knew better. We knew to stay in the back half of the bus.

When the bus stopped in town for lunch, we had to go 'round to a little back window, and the whites would go inside. I don't remember ever sitting at a table. The rest rooms were the same way, colored and white. The other colored people on the trip had maybe traveled before, and knew how to do this. But it was a new experience for us, 'cause we just never got out around in town. No more than to the movies, and there we knew it was upstairs for the blacks and downstairs for the whites. Wasn't that funny—we'd sit up and they'd sit down.

Things weren't much better when we got to California. My first impressions were terrible! We lived in this one-room trailer. One room, honest, and no facilities—no running water, no inside toilet. And boy, when we first got here, it rained every day. We had twelve people in our family, and we all lived in that trailer. Four of us went to work at the Kaiser shipyards. Some of us worked swing shift, or graveyard, while mother was home all the time with the six young kids. We'd take turns sleeping, sharing the beds.

There was not one street out where we lived in North Richmond. The bus would come out there only once a day. So we walked to the shipyards most of the time. There were only colored living in North Richmond until they built the war housing.

It was not much better than home, but at least we had jobs and were making some money. ☐

"Jim Crow" restrictions prevailed at the Greyhound Bus Terminal in Washington, D.C. Crowds mixed before boarding the bus, but waiting rooms and buses were strictly segregated. Not until the civil rights movement of the sixties were many of the Jim Crow customs eradicated.
*John Vachon, Library of Congress*

Wanita Allen and her daughters
Frances and Shirley in the 1940's.

## "I felt like I had just as much right to work as they did."

### Wanita Allen — foundry worker — Detroit, Michigan

I heard they were recruiting women to train to work in the defense plants, and I was coming to Detroit from Lansing, Michigan, whenever I wasn't busy and learned my way around. I met a fellow, and he says, "Why would you be there doing housework when you can get this training at Murray Auto Body to be a riveter. You'll make three times the amount of money you're making." I had these two children and my husband and I had been separated about seven or eight years, so I said, well, this is what I need.

So I came down here and went out to Murray Body to get in the training program. I didn't have any problem getting in the training program. They said you have to have 300 hours to get a job in the plant, and I got my 300, 400, going on 500 hours, and was learning blueprint and everything else, but still no job. They would come in from the plant proper to pick women who'd maybe been there just a couple of days on the training program, and they would put them to work. But they were white women.

They were discriminating and just hiring white women and not hiring black women. I felt like I had just as much right to work as they did, and they had jobs and they had children and I had children. It just made me mad. They were deliberately discriminating. I've been running into it all my life.

So, one day the UAW committeeman from Murray Body came into the plant and he started talking to the different black women and asking them, how many hours they have — haven't they called you to come into the plant? So, we told him no. He says, "We have a suit against the company for discrimination, but I need one of you women to work with me so we can kind of break this down, to get you women in." Everybody said, no, if you work with them, you're not going to get a job yourself. But I said, "Well, I'll take the chance."

He wanted me to go in and ask for a job first, and just let him know who I spoke to and what they told me. I did that and they said, "Well, we're just not hiring now. But just leave your name and address and we'll call you."

The next day the comitteeman says, "Go right back and ask them again. Ask them *why* they're not hiring." So I did that, and he said, "Well, we don't have restrooms set up for the black women yet." So I said, "Couldn't we use the same restroom?" And he says, "No, we're going to have restrooms for the black and for the white, and as soon as we get the restrooms set up, we'll let you know." So I took his name and I reported that.

So the committeeman said, "O.K. you go in tomorrow, and if he says he's not hiring today, just take your lunch and have a seat and just wait. If they hire anybody at all, we want to know it." So I sat there all that day, and he says, "I told you we're not hiring, there's no point in you sitting there." But I said, "Oh, it's O.K., I'm waiting for someone in the plant, I'll just wait here." I wouldn't leave. They didn't hire anybody all that day while I was sitting there.

The next day the union steward said, "We want you to go back in there, and if you see other women in there, get up and take a break. And if you get a chance to talk to some of the women ask them did they get hired." And that's what I did. I waited outside and one white woman came out, and I says, "Oh, you were lucky too, huh, you got hired too. Maybe I'll see you in the plant, what's your name?" And she told me her name, and I told her my name, and I gave this to the union steward, and he said, "Well this is all we want."

So after that, they won the suit and they notified all the black women to come in, so they came in droves and they hired them one by one. □

The National Association for the Advancement of Colored People (NAACP) was among the organizations which challenged racial discrimination during the war. Singer Paul Robeson (second from left) participated in picket lines and sang freedom songs at rallies organizing black workers to fight for "Double Victory" in the auto and shipbuilding industries.
*Schomburg Center Collection, New York Public Library*

*In this passage from* Indignant Heart (*1978*), *auto worker Mathew Ward (the voice of author Charles Denby) recalls the Detroit race riot of 1943, which rocked the entire city and lingers on in the memories of many older citizens today. Race riots, which occurred in Detroit during the Civil War and World War I as well as World War II, were concrete demonstrations of the frustrations felt by blacks as they confronted racism while laboring in industry for the war effort.*

*The first-person narrative voice of this excerpt is traditional in Afro-American literature. The style has been used by many writers to express the personal impact of political conflict.*

## "Why can't we swim in the pool with whites if we're going to fight a war and die with them?"

The Detroit riot broke out in June 1943, on a Sunday afternoon. The riot actually broke out two weeks before, in the Eastwood Amusement Park on Gratiot and Eight Mile Road. Both Negroes and whites attended the park but Negroes were not admitted to the swimming pool. Some jitterbug kids had been drafted and were going into the army in a week. At the park, they were talking among themselves:

"Why can't we swim in the pool with whites if we're going to fight a war and die with them?"

They pulled off their clothes and got in the pool. The manager and some other whites rushed out and a big fight started. The police force came and closed off the area. They turned the streetcars back and sent away all the cars and people. The fight was quelled.

The following Sunday I was visiting Mrs. Gordon. One of her grandsons was telling about the fight. He said they were going to go swimming at Eastwood and that they would swim in any pool. They had to go to the war and they were going to accept their equality before going, and not after, when they might all be dead. He told me that there was going to be a big race riot in the city soon. The tension was for it and it wouldn't be long in coming.

I talked to Mrs. Gordon until about eleven o'clock, and then went on home. I lived on Harper Street. About three o'clock in the morning I heard a lot of shooting, cars running fast and glass breaking.

I shared a room with Wide Modden, a very religious man.

He was a deacon. Just as I dozed back to sleep he ran in, jerked the covers off, and said, "Get up. Get up at once. Get in the streets, there's a big race riot going on. Some white man just threw a Negro woman and her baby off the Belle Isle Bridge into the river." He said several Negroes and many whites had been shot and killed. "They just killed one white down on the corner."

All the time he was talking he was getting his shotgun out of the closet and putting in shells. I was pretty frightened. All I asked was if anyone had saved the woman and baby.

He said he didn't know, he didn't think they had been found yet. "Get up, man. What in hell you waiting for?"

He spoke in a vicious tone, put the shotgun on his arm and headed for the door. I got to the door and heard some more shots; there were bullets whistling. I didn't have a gun. I thought I'd make a target for someone to shoot, so I turned around and went back to bed.

The next morning I was up early and went out on the front porch. An old man, who lived in the house, was sitting by the steps breaking up bricks.

I asked him what he was doing.

In 1942, fighting erupted at the Sojourner Truth Housing Project in Detroit. Racial violence also broke out in Mobile, Alabama, New York City, Dallas, and Beaumont, Texas.
*Arthur Siegel, Library of Congress*

In 1942, homeowners in northeastern Detroit objected to blacks moving into the new Sojourner Truth project. Black tenants attempting to enter were attacked by a mob, and the Ku Klux Klan burned a cross.
*Arthur Siegel, Library of Congress*

He said he was going to use the bricks in the riot.

I kinda smiled and told him they wouldn't be much good in a riot.

He said, "Never mind, David killed Goliath with a rock. These bricks will come in handy."

The street was so crowded with Negroes that you couldn't see the sidewalk. Everyone was quiet, but every store that was white-owned, in that block, was completely smashed. Many things were in the street, groceries, druggist equipment, dry goods, everything. Nobody was touching the stuff.

With everything so quiet I thought the riot was all over. I went to one man and asked him about going to work.

He said, "You can go if you want to, I'm going to stay here. The Oakland streetcar isn't running but you could catch the Russell bus."

I caught the Russell bus to the crosstown and went to the plant. Many Negroes were missing. It looked as if all the white workers were there. There was no tension in the plant between Negroes and whites. Mainly, the Negroes got in groups themselves and talked about the riot. About eleven o'clock the company began to put up notices in the department telling the workers which route to take home and which streetcars were running.

On the streetcar that evening, there were very few Negroes . . . . When I got off at Hastings there seemed to be more Negroes on the street than in the morning. I spoke to one or two people, saying that I thought the riot was about over.

"Hell, no, man, we're just beginning."

They told me about someone they knew who was shot and killed. They told about this white, or that one, who killed some Negro. One told about a friend of his who was an ex-prize fighter. The police were beating his sister and he rushed up, knocked one of the police down, took away his revolver and killed two policemen. Two other policemen came up and shot the fighter in the head. The blood was very fresh on the sidewalk.

Another man told how the city wouldn't send a wagon out for three or four hours to pick up the dead Negroes. They just let them lie in the street. □

Lack of housing forced many families to live "for the duration" in quonset hut or tiny mobile home communities like this one in Richmond, California. *Dorothea Lange Collection, Oakland Museum*

# EVERYDAY LIFE IN WORLD WAR II

*Rosie the Riveter was the woman who got up early in the morning when it was still dark and went to work and came in smiling, drinking coffee, working hard, finding herself as a new person.*
—Lola Weixel, welder, New York

Just as surely as the war indelibly marked the lives of American soldiers overseas, it altered the lives of the women at home who secured wartime industrial jobs in defense plants. Although the women eagerly took the opportunity to earn better wages and learn new job skills, they in turn were forced to make demanding adjustments in both their work and personal lives.

## Keeping Safe on the Job

Because women entering the wartime workforce were physically smaller and largely untrained, many industries adapted their manufacturing processes to the needs of their newest employees. Short-course training replaced long apprenticeships, and tasks requiring complicated steps were broken down into component parts for the less-experienced women. Machine heights were lowered and the arm-reach required of workers reduced. Some factories installed better lighting and moved to protect workers from the most hazardous chemicals and machines.

Industrial safety nevertheless continued to be a severe problem. While combat abroad killed some 500,000 brothers, husbands, sons, and friends, wartime industrial deaths, according to an Office of War Information report in early 1944, totalled some 37,600 workers—7,500 more than killed in combat before D-Day on June 6 of that year. Industrial mishaps, according to the same report, also permanently disabled 210,000 Americans and temporarily disabled another 4,500,000, about 60 times the number of military wounded and missing at that date.

Jobs were not safe. Women were "too delicate" to go to war or do dangerous things, but they would let us be blown up sifting gunpowder. Every last one of us who worked in that department was a woman, and it was very, very dangerous.
—Margaret Wright, munitions worker

Today, ongoing health problems haunt former wartime shipyard workers who suffer from "white lung," an abestos-caused lung ailment frequently leading to cancer.

Better wartime housing was frequently available only to white workers.
*Dorothea Lange Collection, Oakland Museum*

### Finding Housing and Child Care

Occasionally, the companies' accommodations to women workers extended to their needs beyond the shopfloor and shipyard. In Portland, Oregon, for example, Kaiser Shipyards initiated a day care center for its working mothers. On-site industrial credit unions and carpooling networks were also established in some plants to enable workers to reduce time required for "personal" business. These measures, it was calculated, would increase on-the-job satisfaction and productivity. However, such special concessions were rare.

Shipyard workers such as Gladys Belcher, a widow who moved with three children from her farm in Missouri to Richmond, California, or Margaret Wright, who traveled from Detroit to Los Angeles with her child, found it almost impossible to secure housing in the booming wartime production centers. Only one million new units of housing were built nationwide during the entire war, and some 20–40 percent of the two million workers and families who migrated north and west for war work lacked adequate housing for the duration. Many spent uncomfortable months living without plumbing, heat, and running water in tents, chicken coops, and abandoned buildings until permanent accommodations could be found. Then they moved—perhaps with two or three other families—into crowded quarters. Women working second and third shifts tried to sleep with noisy children who had no place to play, and crying babies awoke other babies through the thin walls of "temporary" housing. Dorothy Haener, who worked at the Ford Bomber Plant during the war, remembers how southerners who were recruited to Detroit with promises of good wages and modern housing found that:

> When they got there the housing that was built was pretty much firewood shacks. It was very quickly put together, and you had these people right on top of you, children and families just packed in these places.

In addition to cramped housing, women and men migrating to wartime industrial centers also experienced the unexpected emotional effects of their physical dislocation. Severed were the traditional networks of extended family and friends which had provided economic and emotional support in times of crisis. Gone were the familiar faces and places, the shared histories of the old neighborhoods. Instead, there were new ethnic groups, urban and rural people jumbled together in instant cities frequently popping up in the middle of nowhere.

Particularly trying for women who had packed up and moved was the absence of family and friends who had provided ongoing child care—without question and without pay. Unable to find daytime care for her children and afraid of leaving them unattended, single mother Wanita Allen finally sent her child to a boarding school in the Midwest. Lyn Childs left her daughter with her mother in Los Angeles while she worked at the Richmond shipyards:

> I was going into a new community and I didn't want to bring my child with me. There was no

Mobile homes housed millions of Americans who moved to communities where housing was unavailable. *Russell Lee, Library of Congress*

place for me to put her. When I came up, my husband and I lived in a room in a hotel for a number of years before we could begin to get an apartment or a house to live in. Many women went through the same thing.

Despite the cost-plus contract system which virtually guaranteed that industry would be reimbursed for expenses for employees' services like child care, business owners rarely bothered to make these accommodations which would have considerably eased the everyday burdens on their employees.

### Conflicts on the Home Front

Some women war workers found their family lives completely changed because the size of their new paychecks challenged traditional female-male roles. They were now away from home and had less time to care for their husbands' needs. Clovis Walker's husband continually urged her to quit her job at the Kaiser Shipyard in Richmond, California, and finally hid her leather welder's apron and boots so she couldn't report to work. Although she eventually gave up her shipyard job as he wished, she resented his attempt to run her life, and when they visited his family back east, she "just left him there."

Black singer Huddy Ledbetter recognized the pressures created by women's new economic and even social independence. Describing how he came to write a song about it, "Leadbelly" recalled,

When I was out in California the boys told me, "Ledbetter, the women are working on that defense and they's making lots of money, just quitting their husbands." I met a man out there say, "Ledbetter, you know one thing, I come out here with my wife and you know she done quit me." I say, "Well." He say, "Well, look, every payday come her check is big as mine." I say, "Well." He says, "Well, look, every Saturday she putting her money in the bank." I say, "What then?" He say, "Well, look, can't you make up a song?"

So, "Leadbelly" wrote a song, the "National Defense Blues":

Welders, shipfitters, and electrician's helpers formed the Moore's Shipyard women's glee club which met and rehearsed during lunch hours. *Oakland* (California) *Tribune*, 1942.

I had a little woman, working on that national
  defense,
I had a little woman, working on that national
  defense,
That little woman act just like she did not have
  no sense.

Just because she was working, making so
  much dough,
Just because she was working, making so
  much dough,
That woman got to say she did not love me no
  more.

Every payday would come—her check was big
  as mine,
Every payday would come—her check was big
  as mine,
That woman thought that defense was gonna
  last all time.

That defense is gone, just listen to my song,
That defense is gone, just listen to my song,
Since that defense is gone, that woman done
  lost her home.

I will tell the truth and it's got to be a fact,
I will tell the truth and it's got to be a fact,
Since that defense is gone that woman lose her
  Cadillac.

### Feeding and Clothing the Family

For women who were able to hold their families together, life was far from simple—with or without a good paycheck. Shortages made household duties more time-consuming, especially after essential household appliances such as refrigerators, stoves, vacuum cleaners, and water heaters vanished from the stores. Many women who didn't own washing machines had to wash their families' clothing by hand. When soap became scarce, they made their own. New clothing, which was rationed, seemed to fall apart even before it was home from the store, and baby clothing, diapers, and toys were rarely available.

Food shortages plagued already busy work-

Although the definition of women's work changed during the war, family chores often remained women's sole responsibility. "Even if we weren't working the same shifts, I fixed dinner and left it where it would be convenient for him to get it" (Margaret Wright, ammunitions worker). *Howard Lieberman, Library of Congress*

ing mothers who spent long hours in line, ration coupons in hand, in order to buy small amounts of meat, coffee, sugar, and eggs. Winter weather brought shortages of fresh fruit, vegetables, and milk, and busy urban women began raising "Victory Gardens" and canning fresh produce.

Resourceful women made the best of difficult times. Unable to wait in long lines for rationed goods, some women collected co-workers' ration coupons and purchased items for the entire group while they in turn met her production quota. However, the difficulties of being both workers and wives-and-mothers were stressful for everyone.

The wartime "double day" meant long, hard hours at the plant followed by cleaning, cooking, and child care. *Marjory Collins, Library of Congress*

Rush, rush, rush, until you get through with everything—get dinner over with and get your washing out and iron a few pieces and try to clean up your house—by the time I got in bed it was almost time to get up in the morning. It just got to be too much.

—Wanita Allen, foundry worker
and single mother

When both wife and husband worked, women continued to carry most of the housework responsibilities.

When your husband came home, you know, he propped his feet up and got a can of beer while you fixed dinner, or even if we weren't working the same shifts you fixed dinner and left it where it would be convenient for him to get it.

—Margaret White, munitions worker

## Sharing Work

For many women, working together in a factory or yard during the war was nevertheless a liberating experience.

Instead of working alone all the time, like you do in domestic work, I was always with a bunch of other women. We had lunch together, we helped each other with our jobs. It was sort of a comradely thing, and it was very nice. Also, we rode back and forth with each other, so we made many new friends that you don't when you're working in an isolated job by yourself.

—Margaret Wright

Even gas rationing and the shortage of automobiles had unexpected social benefits. Factory and shipyard workers carpooled or, more frequently, rode the erratic public transportation system together.

It was on the bus that we learned about everyone, everything that was going on. You couldn't read about it; the newspaper didn't print it. There were things happening in every plant, and by the time you got across town, you

Shipyard workers kept informed not only by reading the newspaper. "On the bus we learned about everything. By the time you got across town, you learned about who had walked out and where and why and what everybody was feeling about it" (Jessie Glaberman, assemblyline worker). *Ann Rosener, Library of Congress*

learned about who had walked out and where and why, and what everybody was feeling about it.

—Jessie Glaberman,
assemblyline worker

Despite the government's wartime control of the media, then, women found a way to keep informed about each other's personal lives and the political events around them. Sharing wartime hardships and the strains of a "double day," helping each other learn new skills, feeling proud to be doing valued work, and being financially independent had been the essence of these women's new lives. ☐

*Aircraft worker Gertrude Pennington was pleased to find a good job in a defense plant. She enjoyed the money, the independence, and the good times with her co-workers, but she also had problems with her husband who resented her absence from home.*

### Gertrude Pennington — aircraft worker
### Lockheed Aircraft, Los Angeles, California

**"I said to my husband, 'I got a job.' He was outraged."**

We lived back in Indiana before the war. My husband did well in his job, but he had a weakness for gambling and drinking. He was blowing all his money. Finally I got fed up and wrote to my mother. She said I should just leave. So I moved out to California, where she was, with my two kids, and pregnant with the third. That was about the middle of 1941.

When I got here, I wrote to my husband and said I wasn't coming back. But I still needed money from him for the kids. I hadn't ever had a real job in Indiana, there weren't any for girls my age. I got a job in a coffee shop out here, but my mother made me quit right away because the boss got too chummy with me. So when my husband moved out here, I really hoped he'd turn over a new leaf. Things were better for a little while, but he soon went back to his old ways.

Then the war broke out. My husband was forever buying these adventure, derring-do cowboy magazines, and reading stuff about World War I. So when they announced the bombing of Pearl Harbor, I thought, "Oh, no, here we go again, he's going to be off to the war." We figured my brother-in-law and husband would both enlist. But then my husband decided he wouldn't, that he'd just stay with us. There was still an awful lot of friction, since he was so unreliable. He would just go off and gamble on paydays.

When they started talking about women getting jobs, I figured the way things were going in my house, I'd have to get something. A neighbor of mine worked at Douglas, and told me they were hiring women. I'd told him that I'd never worked in a factory, but he said they didn't care. And he said if I had trouble finding a babysitter, his wife could watch my kids.

So I went down to the employment office, and they sent me down to work at Lockheed on 7th and Santa Fe. They took my picture and my fingerprints, and told me to come

Two young women war workers windowshop in downtown Richmond.
*Dorothea Lange Collection, Oakland Museum*

In defense-work towns like Richmond, traffic ebbed and flowed with the change of factory shifts. Military shipbuilding brought boom times for small businesses in the communities as well.
*Dorothea Lange Collection, Oakland Museum*

back that same night. I'd asked to work graveyard so someone could stay with the kids at night.

When I got home, I said to my husband, "I got a job."

"You got *what?*" He was really outraged.

"I'm going to work tonight," I said.

"Like hell you are," he retorted.

"I'm going to," I said, "and you be sure to get home by 10:00 if you're at the bar, 'cause that's when I'm leaving."

I told my neighbor, "I'm going, because if I give up now, that's it."

"Don't worry," she said."I'll keep an eye on the house, and if I see him go home, I'll know he's there. Otherwise I'll go over at midnight and check." So I went. He must have been watching the house to see if I'd really go. After that he didn't speak to me for a week! He'd go out every evening, and the minute I'd leave he'd come to the house.

The second week I got a paycheck and came in and waved it under his nose, and said, "Take a good look at it, it's the first paycheck I ever had."

He sat there for a while, and then he said, "I don't suppose you'd loan me some of that?" So I did. After the paychecks got to be regular, he didn't squawk so much. He didn't like it, but he didn't squawk.

Soon after that, though, he moved out. Our marriage was all but dead. He'd come by sometimes to see the kids. One time he took them to a park, and my son Butch almost drowned in the lake because he wasn't paying attention.

I worked six nights a week. I used to come home in the morning, and then started cleaning the house. I'd get the kids off to nursery school, then wash, iron, and go to the store, and finally fall into bed around noon. I'd set the alarm for 4:00, get up, run over to the nursery and get the kids, rush them through supper and get them to bed. Then a girl came over to watch them at night while I went to work.

All the women where I lived worked and had kids. Most of them worked in war plants and had the same problems I did, keeping an eye on the kids, buying groceries and paying bills. The woman next door had three kids, and worked part time. In the next apartment was another woman, with five kids and a husband in the service. There were very few men.

We all pitched in to help each other out. If you were going

Women war workers enjoy a lunch break at the Bethlehem Fairfield shipyards in Baltimore.
*Arthur Siegel,Library of Congress*

Wartime work clothes were made of heavy cloth with room for shoulder, back, and leg movement and pockets to hold tools and personal items. Cotton coverall jumpsuits, which cost about $4, were available at most downtown retail shops.
*National Archives*

to the store, people would ask you to get things for them. We each did our own cooking, but often on Saturday nights we would sit outside together and talk over a bottle of wine. Mostly women talked about their jobs, and about what would happen when their husbands came back home. They all knew there was going to be a battle, now that they'd gotten used to having their own paychecks, to being independent. There was more than one argument, in fact several divorces were caused by the men coming home and thinking they were the law of the land. My sister had that experience. When her husband came home, he thought everything would fall into line like before, when he was the sole voice of authority. But it didn't work out that way at all. The kids had gotten used to going to her for permission, and she was used to handling the car, and paying the bills. This wasn't such a problem for me and some other women, those of us who had shaky marriages from the beginning.

One time they came up with this jamboree session at the Plantation Club for people at the plant where I worked. All the girls were going, and I wanted to be a part of it too. I asked what people were gonna wear—"Slacks?"

"No," they said. "The girls really dress up." I had no dresses, just slacks, snoods, blouses, and flat-heeled shoes. So I went down to Sweldon's and bought this two-piece

Raising a Baby on *Shifts*

Mother works nights. The Army wife who shares her home
works days. Between shifts they take care of war baby Billy

By JANE LYNOTT CARROLL

Wartime magazines featured articles
dealing with pressing issues facing
women war workers.
*Ellen Kaiper Collection, Oakland*

tunic dress—emerald green with dark lace. I splurged, and got a new hat—a fisherman's cloche—and new shoes too.

I'd asked my husband to come over to watch the kids. And my mother dropped by that day too—she hadn't known I was going out. The kids tattled on me, they said, "Wait till you see Mom's new dress!" Then the fight was on. My mother was shocked over the price of the hat, and my husband thought I'd flipped my lid.

Somehow I got out of there, and ten of us jammed into a car. The ballroom was loaded with people. It was sort of a release. Most of the girls had gone out and bought clothes for this special occasion. Our lead man came and sat with us for awhile, and there were a lot of men from the different plants.

Count Basie's band was there. We had a table fairly close to the floor, and somehow I got to talking to Basie. He was very friendly, and full of fun. He said to me, "Are you a riveter?"

"No, I said,"but my sister's name is Rosie." We got to kidding around, and then he sang that song called "Rosie the Riveter," while I sat on the piano bench with him. I really had a wonderful time.

We had another big row when I got home. My mother thought I was neglecting the kids. Everyone was mad at me for going. But I wasn't that concerned about the fuss they made. By this time, you know, it was late in the war, and women were making more money, and we were starting to manage our own affairs.

Not long after this, my husband got tangled up with a gal, and ran up a big bill buying her clothes. They tried to make me pay for the bill, saying I was legally responsible. I got some help from a counselor at work, but in the end I still had to pay.

That was when I filed suit for divorce. I won, and the judge gave me a $25 weekly allowance for the children that my husband was supposed to pay. I wasn't making enough to pay for a babysitter, groceries, clothes, and dentist bills. So I tried to make damn sure I'd get the money from him every week for the kids. If he had the money, I could get it, but he'd hit the bars or the horses the minute he got paid. A lot of times by the time he'd come by the house with money he would be either desperate or broke. Sometimes it wouldn't be $25 but $15, and some weeks he would miss paying altogether.

He missed just once too often. So one payday, I packed my kids in the car, after putting their oldest clothes on them, so they'd look their worst. I put on my old jeans myself, and we drove over to the plant where my husband worked. I parked the car just a little past the plant gate, and stuck butcher paper all over the back end of it. I wrote on it, in big letters, "My husband hasn't paid child support and we need the money." I hung a sign around Butch's neck which said, "I need new shoes." He didn't want to wear it, and he started crying, but I was so mad, I said, "Either you wear that or I'm gonna blister your rear end." The girls wore signs too, saying, "My dad hasn't given mom any money."

After this was all set up, the guys started coming out of the plant. And they'd never seen anything like it. My God, I created a riot. But it worked. My husband came through the gate, saw that car and his three kids, with Butch standing in front of the car with tears rolling down his cheeks— wearing old clothes, his toes poking out of his shoes. My husband was so mad! His face turned bright red, then as white as death. The other men were all looking, and nudging each other, waiting to see what would happen.

We went over to a place right near the plant where you could buy beer, cash checks, and bet on the horses. Half of the men followed us in, and the kids came too. He owed me child support for three weeks. I said, "How much can you give me?

"$25," he said.

I said, "That's not enough." And everybody was there watching, you know—I could feel the eyes burning in the back of my head. So I got about $50 from him. Then I said, "Do you want me to come back to the plant next week?"

"On, no, no!" he said. That's the way I got at him. You just had to nail him. ☐

Children of women war workers saw their mothers change to unconventional clothing, take up unfamiliar tools, and go to work in new places. *Tampa* (Florida) *Tribune, National Archives*

# "They were all so close together, it didn't seem decent."

*In this selection from the novel* The Dollmaker *(1949), Harriet Arnow describes a rural Applachian woman's first night in a city. Gertie Nevels has moved her children to Detroit, where her husband Clovis works in a defense plant. Through the thin walls of their crowded shack, she tries to interpret the confusing noises made by her neighbor Sophronie, a woman, she learns, who also works in a factory.*

The evening in the hot, overcrowded, noise-laden place seemed endless. She answered questions about back home, learned that Sophronie's man, Whit Meanwell, worked in the same Flint plant as Clovis, though on a different job and shift. She wanted to ask Clovis questions: how much did they owe, how much was the interest on the debts for the car and the house plunder, where was the school, and how far away? But the radio was on, and she talked but little.

As soon as the children were asleep, Clovis had no thought for answering questions. Amos had been put to bed on the cot in the middle room, so that Gertie and Clovis were alone in the room beside the kitchen. Still, she was conscious of the restless sleep of the children on the other side of the thin walls. They were all so close together it didn't seem decent. The whole place wasn't as big as either of the two main rooms at the Tipton Place.

She shut her eyes and tried to think that she was there when Clovis fell quickly into a deep, satisfied sleep. She drowsed and dreamed of pines talking. The talking rose, became the roar of a fast through train, its screeching whistle rising above the roar as it neared the through street. This was followed at once by the tumultuous sound of its passing, so close it seemed in the very house. [Her children] Amos and Cassie screamed out in fright, then as the sounds subsided they sank gradually into a whimpering half-sleep. There remained only the quiverings—the windows, the steel springs of the bed, the dishes, a chair touching the wall.

There came at last a silence so complete she could hear the ticking of the clock under the bed, and the snoring of Sophronie's children behind the wall of the girl's bedroom . . . . The feeling that had followed her at times since she had got on the train came back in the silence—she had forgotten something, something very important. But what? She was sorting out the things she'd left behind when she found herself lifted on one elbow listening.

Someone was moving about on the other side of the wall. She heard running water, the soft thud of a pot going over the gas flame, the creak and slam of an icebox door—breakfast-getting sounds. Soon she heard the opening and closing of the outside door, and whoever it was did not come back. He had not taken time to eat his breakfast. He was most likely the husband of that Sophronie in the sleazy nightgown. She was too lazy to get up and cook breakfast.

She drowsed, but sleep enough never came to drown the strangeness of the bed or the closeness of the air. It seemed only a little while before she found herself listening again. A singing it was in the alley now. Tipsy he was, and a tenor, "They'll be pie in a sky--" A woman's voice cut him off, something like the girl Maggie's, but near crying, "Please, Joseph, please. Du neighbors--".

"Quitcha tucken," the man said, and a door on the other side of the alley slammed.

"Tucken." What was "tucken," she wondered. Then the door next to her own was opened quietly, but slammed shut so loudly that Clovis turned in his sleep. She heard the opening of the oven door, the little whoosh of the lighting gas, then the opening and closing of the icebox door. A chair was pulled out followed by the hissing sound of the cap jerked off a bottle of something fizzy like pop. She heard a chair tip back against the wall, so close through the thinness seemed like she could feel it. She could see the man's chair leaning against the wall, his cold feet warming in the oven, as he drank from the bottle. She heard the soft clink of glass on steel as he put it down. But where had he been and why, at this time of night? She sat straight up in bed with wonder and surprise when the voice came, low, more like a sigh than a voice, "Oh, Lord, that moven line," for the voice was a woman's voice, Sophronie's.

The sounds on the other side of the wall or her own abrupt movement awakened Clovis enough that he mumbled sleepily: "Don't be afeared, Gert. The door's locked good."

"Oh, I ain't afeared," she whispered. "It's that Sophronie. Why, she's jist got in home."

He clamped one ear against the pillow, put an arm over the other. "When else would a woman on the three-tu-twelve shift git home?" ☐

Some families managed to raise down-payments for hastily built homes in federally sponsored housing projects.
*Dorothea Lange Collection, Oakland Museum*

*In this excerpt from "I Looked Over Jordan," a short story by Ernie Brill (1980), Dr. Middlebrook talks with Moses Green, a black shipyard worker who has entered the hospital with severe chest pains. Green suffers from asbestosis, a deteriorative disease caused by asbestos dust in the lungs which claims thousands of lives annually and affects millions more. Many former World War II shipyard workers have died or will die from the disease.*

# "Patient has worked constantly around asbestos."

[Dr.] Middlebrook opened the [Moses Green's] chart, paused at the article stuck inside, and cursed. He wished that Laura, the Industrial Claims interviewer, had never given his intern the article. Why complicate things? They all knew how terrible asbestosis was. Goddamn pushy bitch. No wonder. Laura was from Detroit. He'd never met a patient person from Detroit. She knew her stuff, though—knew it, he admitted, grudgingly, better than most interns and residents. And, admitting deeper, better than most staff doctors. A clerk with a B.A. But she was definitely pushing, going beyond her bounds, xeroxing articles. Middlebrook pushed the article aside, and thumbed through the chart.

Moses Green. Middlebrook stared at the Emergency Room sheet shorthand: 61 yr. old BM with acute sob, chest pains. He turned the page to Laura's neatly typed, fully worded industrial interview:

> Sixty-one year old black man presented to Emergency Room via ambulance in severe distress with acute shortness of breath and severe chest pains radiating to shoulders, arms, and back. Patient has worked on docks and shipyards for over forty years: 1930's and 40's (early) New Orleans, Louisiana, and Mississippi (Biloxi, Pascagoula). Patient an excellent historian. In Mississippi patient worked as ships-caler and laborer in enclosed spaces in the holds of various-ships, as well as in various engine and boiler rooms installing insulation and laying gratings. Both the installation material and gratings contained asbestos used for fireproofing. Patient claims there was little ventilation and constantly "clouds of white dust." Often dust was so thick patient could not see his co-workers fifteen to twenty feet away. Patient claims they were given masks at times, but that these masks did not prove adequate for any great or even consistent period of time. Patient claims that the dust was "all over the place," often remaining in the workclothes of himself and his fellow employees.
>
> Patient worked in the Richmond-Oakland area from

1940-1944, when he was drafted into the army. Since returning he has worked in the Hunter's Point shipyard from 1946 (approximately) to the present. Patient has worked constantly around asbestos, as well as in hot, smoky environment for over forty years.

After staring at the pathology report, Middlebrook closed the chart. He gritted his teeth. Mike rightly called Mose Green the question man. Moses reminded the doctor of a bulldog: slow, but once the teeth sank in, forget letting go. He was unlike Middlebrook's other patients, who growing obsessed with their illnesses, became pathetic experts, writing elaborate letters documenting every little creak and pimple. No, Moses was something else Middlebrook had rarely encountered. During the hospitalization, Green asked if he could "read up on it." The surprised intern told him Mose planned a trip to the library. At first Middlebrook encouraged it—give Green a focus. Soon Middlebrook found it distasteful. The man obviously had limited reading skills, reading with his finger, following words. Why struggle and strain in a library? Irked, Middlebrook felt his medical judgement doubted. True, he always wanted his patients informed, yet Moses presented a different dimension with his unending drawl, "Can you run that by me again?" asking questions when Middlebrook was behind

"Industrial casualties between Pearl Harbor and Jan. 1 of this year [1944] aggregated 37,600 killed, or 7,500 more than the military dead, and 210,000 permanently disabled and 4,500,000 temporarily disabled, or sixty times the number of military wounded and missing (*New York Times*, January 21, 1944). *Library of Congress*

This woman worked in a steel mill in Gary, Indiana, as a panman, mixing sealing mud for casting iron. Many defense plant jobs were unhealthy and dangerous.
*OWI, National Archives*

schedule with other patients to see, never being able to spend much time with his patients in the hospital and the clinic. Middlebrook also felt he had bent over backwards for Moses, genuinely liking the man, feeling bad for him.

He suddenly noticed the clock. He'd spent five minutes thumbing through a chart he knew by heart. Cursing himself, he strode toward Room B, and pulled back the curtain.

"Hello, Moses. How are you?" Middlebrook smiled, sticking out his hand.

"Fine," Moses said, shaking Middlebrook's hand, "fine, Doc."

"Your, uh, breathing machine working o.k.?"

"Oh yeah. I got the hang of it."

"You had it when you left."

"Mazin' little machine," Mose said politely, staring at the doctor, trying to read the news. Middlebrook tried to stare at Moses' forehead, and lost as if fought by a stare made of magnets. His eyes locked into Green's, and Moses, staring him straight in the eyes, knew.It was forever if it was less than thirty seconds.'

"Sit down Mose."

"I'll stand if you don't mind."

Middlebrook hid behind the chart. Despite his shirt and the white coat over it, he felt nude. He took a deep breath, and plunged.

"Your report came back positive."

"Positive? The piece of lung you took?"

"It's malignant."

As if blind, feeling for a chair somewhere, Mose pulled it over and sat down. "Lord." He breathed deep, as if he could feel by breathing the place where the cancer lived. He breathed short, labored, wondering what exact part of him breathing was full of that . . . A great urge gripped him—to tear off all his clothes, reach inside his lungs, and grab that malignancy out—get a hold of it—every last bit of it and tear it outta there—go deep as need be to get it all out, like blood leeches in swamp water, he wanted to get it offa himself—he shuddered—where else was it, how far was it in—he shuddered and smelled his fear—strong, sour.

"Often," he heard the doctor saying, "often it develops in patients with asbestosis. Not always, but often." □

# CHILD CARE FOR WORKING MOTHERS

*The government provided child care centers that were really well run. . . . I would get the kids up at 5:00 a.m., take them to the nursery in their night clothes, then I had to be at work by 6:00 a.m.*
—Jean Maddox, milk truck driver, Oakland

*Child care? I never heard of any, you know, where I could take my children anyway. I had to put my daughter in boarding school. I ran into so many brick walls, keeping her in private homes and everything.*
—Wanita Allen, foundry worker, Detroit

In today's economy most workers' wages fail to keep pace with inflation. As a result, both parents in a family often work to make ends meet and maintain a comfortable living standard. For single parents, locating good day care at an affordable price frequently makes the difference between welfare poverty and family survival.

Finding child care is a frustrating and time-consuming experience for working parents. The few affordable community cooperatives, church-based centers, or federally funded neighborhood programs often have waiting lists and special enrollment qualifications. In addition, parents are sometimes shocked to discover the low-quality attention given at some centers. This sometimes forces them to look again and again for responsible care that meets parents' hours and incomes.

Extensive child care systems exist in many countries where women are fully integrated into the work force—the Scandinavian countries and even the much poorer countries of Eastern Europe. In the United States, however, some people still maintain that child care is "un-American" or that it spells the end of the family. During World War II, however, child care programs were part of the nation's victory strategy, and although far from adequate in numbers, they enabled many mothers to join the work force with the assurance that their children would be adequately cared for.

## Child Care During World War II

Three main types of child care were available during the war years: federally funded centers, community or church-sponsored centers, and workplace centers.

*Federally funded centers*—Although some federal aid for child care was available before

(Facing Page)   A few model child care centers like this one in Atlanta offered a variety of play and learning activities. *Marjory Collins, Library of Congress*

1943, the only major government commitment came under the Lanham Act of that year, which created a general fund for wartime community services. Over the objections of Congressman Fritz G. Lanham (Dem., Texas), Congress apportioned some of these funds to day care. By 1945, the government-sponsored centers provided care for 100,000 children across the country, but this was only about one-tenth of the children with working mothers who needed day care services, Federal funding was withdrawn after the war, and most centers closed.

*Community sponsored centers*—Many community child care centers, sponsored by churches or charities, were unpublicized. In Detroit, some racially mixed centers were sponsored by the Merrill-Palmer School, an early childhood education research center, but in many communities referral agencies often discouraged racially integrated centers. Some mothers refused to use community or settlement house facilities because they identified them with accepting "relief" or charity, a prejudice carried over from the 1930's.

*Workplace centers*—During the war, employers sometimes provided child care facilities for their employees. They did so because the cost-plus contract system enabled them to pass on their expenses to the Department of War as part of the costs of manufacturing ships, tanks, military clothing, or bombs. In Portland, Oregon, the exemplary child care center run by Kaiser Shipyard was open on all three shifts to accommodate hundreds of children. It also offered a convenient carry-out meal service for mothers which helped them save hours in shopping and meal preparation. A tank plant in Peoria, Illinois, and a tent and uniform manufacturing shop (formerly a men's clothing factory) in Cleveland, Ohio, also had in-plant child care centers.

## Not Enough Centers for Everyone

The major drawback of World War II child-care facilities was simply that there were too few of them. As a result, many women had to rely on old networks of support to get them through these difficult years. Before she moved to the West Coast, for example, Margaret Wright recalls,

> I didn't worry about child care because the black community always had a very strong extended family concept. Even with just friends, if I wanted to go downtown or something, I didn't even have to ask my friend would she keep my kid. I would just send my kid over there, it was that kind of relationship.

For thousands of families who pulled up roots and moved north and to the coasts to take defense industry jobs, however, these neighborhood connections had been severed. Accordingly, families were forced to make do with whatever arrangements they could find, or

*Library of Congress*

Longer store hours in some industrial communities gave women defense workers a chance to shop for food, another facet of women's double day.
*Russell Lee, Library of Congress*

leave their children behind with close relatives when they had to move.

On occasion, new family arrangements were developed to accommodate the need for child care. Parents frequently took jobs on different shifts, creating new strains on their relationships. Although men might shoulder some responsibility for domestic needs, more often than not women made all arrangements for the care of their children, while continuing to do all the housework and work full time. The result was the grueling "double day." As former shipyard worker Clovis Walker remembers, "During the war years, you had to work a double job. You had to work hard and cook dinner and clean house, pick up children, everything."

### Centers Close at War's End

Wartime child care was sponsored by government and industry primarily to gain and maintain high production levels by women workers. As a result, many of the programs on which working women depended were summarily cut off after the war, despite organized attempts in communities and workplaces to keep them going. Child-care parents set up telephone chains, wrote letters, and planned public meetings. For example, in California, some 5,000 Los Angeles parents of pre-school age children rallied to protest the cancellation of funding for child care in 1946, and groups from across the state sent delegations to Sacramento to lobby for extension of child care funding. But these struggles were largely unsuccessful, and unsympathetic legislators cynically stated to the public that mothers merely wanted to park their children in child care centers in order to drink in bars or go to the movies.

For the duration, most women war workers with children held onto their jobs, determinedly juggling long hours at work, child raising, and domestic responsibilities in order to be employed at well-paying work they enjoyed doing. In the years following the war, many of them wanted to continue working and to have access to the facilities that would provide good care for their children. That did not prove to be possible. Today, however, the increasing numbers of women working outside the home for similar reasons of interest and necessity are again making child care a major issue. □

Joyce Maupin and daughter in the 1940's.

# "There was this fine nursery right in the area."

*During the war, Joyce Maupin moved to San Francisco from Seattle and discovered that finding decent housing and good child care was nearly impossible. Finally, she ignored the advice of community agencies which informally sanctioned racially segregated child care facilities and found a place for her daughter in the Booker T. Washington nursery school in San Francisco.*

### Joyce Maupin—laborer
### Bemis Bag Company, San Francisco

Even to get a place to live was very complicated. I remember, when I first came to San Francisco, carrying my daughter Irene in my arms to about 50 hotels. Eventually I did get something, through war housing, but that was because my husband was in the Merchant Marine, and I was on a special priority list. And I had to agree to take the job of cleaning up the halls to get the place.

Then, I tried to find a child care center. Irene had always been in a center, and was very unhappy in the period when we first arrived. Once when she was staying at my mother-in-law's house, she disappeared, and it turned out that she'd wandered off to a child care center—she heard the children playing. They wondered where this strange child had come from!

Finally the war information committee recommended a center to me. It involved taking three trolley cars to get there, and then three more for me to get to work. So I'd spend one day at work and another day traveling the trollies. It was just impossible.

Then I saw a photo of a nursery school that seemed to be in the area I was living in, and I ran into the information center and asked, "What about that one?"

"Oh," they said, "that's just for colored children." It was the Booker T. Washington Nursery School. I looked at the photo again, and a couple of the children in it looked awfully white. So I went over there, and I told them what the War Information Center had told me—that this place was only for colored children.

There were no blacks in the white nursery schools, and they had originally established this nursery school so the black mothers would have a place to take their children, but when white mothers had applied they had decided not to

Some lucky parents with children in child care centers like the Bella Vista Nursery in Oakland were comforted to know that their children's health was protected. This mother worked a graveyard shift and took her daughter to the center while she slept during the day. *Ann Rosener, OWI, Library of Congress*

discriminate. So, that's where Irene stayed until she was old enough for regular school. It was right in my neighborhood, and I could just walk there with her. It was so ridiculous for me to be told I had to go somewhere which involved six trips of transportation, when there was this fine nursery right in the area! □

# PROPAGANDA ON THE HOMEFRONT

*While other girls attend their favorite cocktail bars,*
*Sipping dry martinis, munching caviar,*
*There's a girl who's really putting them to shame.*
*Rosie is her name.*
*All day long whether rain or shine*
*She's a part of the assembly line.*
*She's making history, working for victory,*
*Rosie the Riveter.*
> —Popular 1940's tune, "Rosie the Riveter"

A sometimes hidden but always influential aspect of wartime life was the federal government's efforts to influence the way people viewed the war. Although the majority supported United States involvement after the Japanese attack on Pearl Harbor, the government nevertheless carefully prepared propaganda to use on the home front for the duration. The purpose of this propaganda was to mobilize widespread support for wartime policies and actions.

During World War I, the Creel Committee of Public Information was able to push a "voluntary" censorship program on newspapers. It also mounted a massive propaganda campaign to help sell war bonds, combat absenteeism, and convince people that the war was in their best interests. During World War II, this responsibility was assigned to the Office of War Information.

The Office of War Information (OWI) was a powerful agency whose task was to shape all public information in any way related to the war. This meant that the OWI reviewed or set guidelines for consumer advertisements promoting products ranging from silk stockings to train travel, for feature films and newsreels shown regularly in movie theaters, for posters and billboards, and for articles in newspapers and magazines. (In the movie *The Life and Times of Rosie the Riveter,* the scenes filmed in black and white are OWI-sanctioned material— weekly newsreels such as "The March of Time," documentary shorts on war workers, government recruitment and training films, and even newspaper photos.)

Among the responsibilities given the OWI was the "selling" of the idea that women were able—and indeed obligated—to become involved in war work. The OWI materials also recruited women for war production jobs, persuaded them to sacrifice personal concerns in order to maintain high production quotas, and encouraged them to leave their jobs when the

(Facing Page)   The OWI and the War Manpower Commission conducted advertising campaigns to keep production high. *Dorothea Lange Collection, Oakland Museum*

war ended. On most accounts, the OWI was successful.

## How Propaganda Works

Propaganda contains truth as well as half-truths, exaggerations, and outright lies. Effective propaganda plays into our needs and fantasies and then directs that psychological energy for the purposes for which it has been designed. The manipulation happens as a "hooking" process: our attention is captured on an emotional level, and we are then drawn into believing that the information contained in the propaganda is true. Often, too, propaganda will reintroduce emotional themes in order to move us along from belief to action.

There are many examples of this process in the propaganda sections of the film *The Life and Times of Rosie the Riveter*. The clip from *The Hidden Army*, an OWI film that begins with the actress (playing a wartime worker) waking up at 5:30 a.m. and flopping back into bed, always elicits chuckles of recognition and sympathy from contemporary viewers. Wanting to turn over for another forty winks before going to work is a common human experience. The male narrator of the film then states a half-truth ("some were too tired in the morning to face the assembly line"), insinuates that some women workers wanted wartime paychecks only to buy consumer luxuries, and states finally that the real problem was that "women were not accustomed to the long hours of hard work." Our sympathy has been hooked and twisted into indignation at the selfish, lazy women workers.

By the end of the clever film, women are being blamed for war casualties. As the story unfolds, absenteeism has caused production shortages which in turn cause the mother and sweetheart to receive a tragic telegram (drama-

"The need for women to replace men in necessary civilian jobs of all kinds," read this wartime advertisement, "is an unusual opportunity for patriotic women everywhere to serve their country. Investigate at your U.S. Employment Office . . . even though you have never worked before." *Photoplay*, September, 1943

WITH SONS AT WAR
...AMERICA NEEDS
WORKERS!

BE A
"FIGHTER-
BACKER"
you can do a lot

Minority workers were rarely pictured in recruitment propaganda campaigns, which appealed to women's sense of responsibility and sacrifice. *Ellen Kaiper Collection, Oakland*

tized with no more dialogue than a sobbing "No!"). When the story concludes by showing a corpse-littered battlefield with the war hero's posthumous military award superimposed over the carnage, most viewers are ready with the narrator to forget at least two important pieces of well-known but never-mentioned information about the wartime defense industry: that there was a high rate of male as well as female absenteeism and that supplies often did not reach the troops on the battlefield because of poor management and distribution, not because women took time off work for family emergencies.

It is the tension between truths and falsehoods that makes propaganda like this so strong in its emotional appeal. The ambivalence of these media messages to the wartime public is an important aspect of the way *The Life and Times of Rosie the Riveter* is structured. As the film develops, the contrast deepens between the personal testimonies of the five women and the myths projected in the newsreels. At the beginning of the film, there is some truth in the black-and-white images of neighborhood recruitment for war work and of women operating heavy machinery. But the distortions are also present in the narrator's patronizing claim, and the accompanying images, of skilled factory work being just like housework. A drill press, he tells us, can be operated "as easily as a juice extractor."

As the film continues, the manipulation becomes more obvious. When the Supervisor of Women Employees, also an actress, takes us on a factory tour to show us women workers "in almost every department in the plant," we are fascinated by the glimpses of women in nontraditional occupations and appreciate the Supervisor's affirmation that "they do a man's job and they can draw a man's pay." But her next remark is an outright lie: "They're doing it safely. They're safer here than in their own homes." Welder Gladys Belcher's testimony about shipyard accidents follows directly to emphasize the enormity of that falsehood.

By the end of the movie, the propaganda-reality contrast is very blatant. The American dream of a secure and serene home life is projected as a glorification of family life and condemnation of women's work outside the home. In a remarkably ambiguous scene, Dr. Marynia Farnham, a career woman, is used as the authority to persuade women that women's participation in the workforce causes unhappiness in family life.

When we see examples of World War II propaganda today, the obvious stylistic differences in the way words and pictures were used, as well as our after-the-fact knowledge about what happened, make it easier to identify attempts to influence our way of thinking. Partial truths and plays on our hopes and fears often seem glaringly obvious. This distance enables us to weigh the message being projected against what we know by our own experience or by history to be true.

It is more difficult to see how the media influences us in our own times. Movies, books, radio, and newspapers obviously can't use every photograph or tell every side of an issue. So they select words, pictures, and ideas, but claim to tell us "objective" truth. In order for us to evaluate their interpretation of an event or policy or product, we need to know who has paid for it to be made, where the facts come from, and what the article or book or movie is trying to encourage us to do—to take or not take certain actions, to think or feel in a particular way, or to buy a product.

### Recruiting Women and Keeping Them in Their Places

At the beginning of World War II, the federal government launched a vigorous campaign to recruit women for war production work. Paul McNutt of the War Manpower Commission assessed his task this way: "Getting these women into industry is a tremendous sales proposition."

But from the beginning, government and the companies knew that women would be needed in heavy industry only as long as the war lasted, and consequently their propaganda pitch was aimed mainly at women's traditional role as helper rather than a new role as worker. Accordingly, government posters, films, and advertisements showed white middle-class housewives laying aside their card games in order to "help out for the duration."

Many former housewives and women who were new to industry did join the workforce, true to the "Rosie" image, but many women came from different backgrounds. Factory owners preferred hiring older women with previous work experience who had older children. As a result, single mothers, minority women, and women who had already been forced to work outside the home as waitresses or domestics or in agriculture and light manufacturing jobs made up the majority of defense workers.

Throughout the war years, however, most popular songs, stories, and magazine articles denied many essential aspects of women war workers' lives. Propaganda frequently emphasized women's patriotic commitment, an appeal only slightly removed from the traditional stereotype of feminine self-sacrifice. One newsreel, for example, showed an attractive actress taking an assembly line job because the nation was "in a jam," and the newsreel narrator further commented, "Somehow that answer pleased us. No sudden emotional urge sent this young woman into war work. No loss of a loved one. No temporary economic embarrassment." That women worked and had previously worked outside the home to support their families, and that they jumped to take war production jobs because they offered better pay and sometimes more meaningful work went largely unrecognized. That the women were often non-white family breadwinners and the victims of discrimination by employers and co-workers also escaped notice in newsreels and magazines.

Sometimes in the popular culture, insights surfaced about women's real situation within the workforce. A view occasionally emerged of women as people who needed to work and even enjoyed the independence of their new economic status. Benny Goodman's jazz band, for

example, played the popular tune, "Minnie's in the Money":

Have you heard that Minnie's in the money?
Take my word that Minnie's in the money.
She hasn't got a guy who's got a diamond mine,
But she's a welder on the old assembly line.
So bless her, sir, Minnie's in the money,
Minnie's in the money, that's fine,
She's helping Uncle Sam to keep his people free.
She's okay, hey, the Minnie's in the do-re-mi.

Another purpose of wartime propaganda was to keep women from making demands on the war production system. A popular jingle sung by Patty Ryan warned:

The day after payday's not the time to relax.
Get on the job and give the Axis the axe.
Time won't wait for you and me,
Don't be an absentee.

Even sanitary napkin advertisements chided women for "feeling blue" when menstruating, because winning victory depended on factory women producing at top efficiency every day.

Popular advertising campaigns sold consumer products as well as the idea of working hard for national defense. Women's magazines such as *McCalls* also urged women to participate in the war effort. *McCalls*, 1944; *Photoplay*, September, 1943

## Absent-ee-minded

**How,** you ask, can you be all-out for Victory on days like this . . . when you feel all in?

That's strange talk . . . coming from *you!* You who were so proud to carry the blow torch for Uncle Sam . . . first in your plant to sign the scroll pledging you'd *stay on the job.*

And now you're telling yourself that girls are different . . . and that one little layoff day won't matter. When you *know* that if it weren't for stay-at-homes, scores more ships . . . tanks . . . bombers would reach our boys!

That's how important it is to learn that loyalty never watches the clock . . . or the calendar! As Marge, your welder friend, said in the locker room—"When a girl takes over a man's work, it's up to her to see it through!"

And then didn't she say—"Trouble is, some girls *still* don't know what a big difference *real comfort* can make. The kind you get from Kotex sanitary napkins." Could be . . . she meant *you!*

### Get Up and GO!

If *millions* can keep going in comfort *every* day, so can you! You'll understand why, when you discover that Kotex is made to stay soft while wearing . . . ever so different from pads that only feel soft at first touch. (None of that snowball sort of softness that packs hard under pressure!)

And to keep your secret *strictly* private . . . to give you confidence and poise . . . Kotex has flat pressed ends that don't show, because they're not stubby. Then, there's a special 4-ply safety center for added protection. So . . . it's not surprising that more girls choose Kotex than all other brands of pads put together! Don't you agree?

Then c'mon . . . hop into those victory togs and help your plant win that precious "E"! You'll deserve an "E" of your own . . . for being an "Everydayer"!

### Keep going in comfort-with Kotex!

**WHY WONDER** about what to do and not to do on "Difficult" days? The bright little booklet "As One Girl To Another" gives you all the angles on activities, grooming, social contacts. Get *your* copy quick! It's FREE! Mail your name and address to P. O. Box 3434, Dept. MW-9, Chicago.

**You can't be too careful!** Fortunately there is a *sure way* to avoid offending. Just sprinkle QUEST, the Kotex Deodorant Powder, on your sanitary pad! Created expressly for this use, QUEST *destroys* odors completely—without retarding napkin absorbency.

(*T. M. Reg. U. S. Pat. Off.)

At war's end, a massive propaganda campaign attempted to persuade women workers to sacrifice their jobs to male workers. Veterans who had accumulated seniority while in the military were rehired, as were many men who had neither served in the armed forces nor worked in war industry. *Ellen Kaiper Collection, Oakland*

This ad for typewriters suggested that "a surprising number of war workers are going to learn to type . . . a skill easy for them to acquire." It continued, "For women who want careers, typing is the opening wedge to the world's most fascinating professions." *Ellen Kaiper Collection, Oakland*

## Propaganda to Send Women Home

The coming of peace will work no unemployment hardships on you. You women have been employed because the armed forces called your husbands, brothers or sons . . . . Each serviceman will get his job back when this war is won. And you women and girls will go home, back to being housewives and mothers again, as you promised to do when you came to work for us. If all industry would adopt this simple policy, there would be no serious post-war problem of unemployment.

—*Bill Jack vs. Adolph Hitler*
March of Time Newsreel

As the end to World War II approached, the newsreels turned their attention to the problem of getting women out of the war production factory jobs they had so eagerly recruited for and filled a few years earlier. Ammunitions worker Margaret Wright remembers that "even the articles in the magazines changed":

You know, during the war they was telling you to cook dishes that you cook quick and get on to work. Now, they were telling you how to cook dishes that took a full day. There were more articles in there about raising your child and the psychological development of your children. They never did mention that, you know, before the war . . . .

The themes of this new kind of official and unofficial propaganda varied, especially as developed in popular magazines, newspapers, and newsreels. Most, however, focused on post-war prosperity, the end of the need for women to work outside the home, and the growing importance of the peacetime consumer economy.

American exploitation of the third world's material and social resources—a major facet of United States foreign policy in the late 1940's and 1950's—was glibly justified in one film image of tattered natives shipping raw materials to America. In that same newsreel, a white American housewife looks toward Armistice this way: "First thing I'm going to do after the war is get a vacuum cleaner. And a maid to run it." Throughout the war, domestic workers were scarce because other jobs were available to poor white and third-world women—Afro-American, Asian American and Latina American. During reconversion, however, these women were pushed out of their wartime jobs in manufacturing or public services and back down into "private service" work at much lower wages and status.

Nevertheless, for the now "average" nuclear family of 2.5 children, unpaid housework and child-rearing were again promoted in popular culture as women's proper pastimes. Advertising used this patriarchal, white, single-income "model" family to compel Americans to acquire new energy-consuming appliances and cars. Buying on credit was encouraged, which made the second family income more and more necessary.

After the war, women who continued to work outside the home were critically portrayed in the popular culture as selfishly and willingly causing divorce, juvenile delinquency, crime, and other problems affecting the post-war population. Complained one newsreel,

> The family was solidly founded on the father as patriarch and breadwinner, and on the mother as cook, housekeeper, and nurse of the children. One of the trends of modern life which has been cited as most disruptive of marriage is the increasing economic independence of women. . . . Everywhere children of working parents are being left without adequate supervision or restraint.

While the divorce rate did climb after the war, the real reason was not only financially independent women but also the return of war-brutalized veterans who had difficulty readjusting to civilian life. Shipyard burner Lyn Childs remembers the painful experience which led to her divorce: "When he came back, he came back shell-shocked, very mean, and started beating on me and other things." As welder Lola Weixel viewed the situation, the tension between husbands and wives was aggravated by the bleak employment prospects in the post-war economy for veterans:

> It wasn't like a dance in the opera. The men came home beat up, the men came home with problems. They gave them free ads in the newspapers looking for jobs, but it was pathetic.

In the media barrage encouraging women war workers to hand over their jobs to male workers, one particularly effective voice was popular psychoanalyst Dr. Marynia Farnham, who co-authored the bestseller *Modern Woman: The Lost Sex* (1942). Urging women to express "love, affection, and surrender," the book and countless articles it inspired accused women who worked of turning into their husbands' rivals and depriving their children of needed love.

Post-war followers of Farnham attempted to expand further the idea that woman's duty was to her species. In 1945, for example, a San

*Ellen Kaiper Collection, Oakland*

Francisco newspaper article by sociologist Willard Waller warned:

> If we are to have an adequate birthrate, we must hear less talk about women's rights and more about their duty to the race. The plain fact is, women do not produce children under the conditions of freedom and equality that have existed in the United States since the last war. . . . Usually the career of a brilliant woman is bought at the cost of an empty nursery. The price is too high.

Nazi ideology had demanded the complete submission of woman to her biological role. In contrast, the wartime recruitment newsreel *The Hidden Army,* released only several years earlier when women had been desperately needed in the labor force, had projected the OWI concept that World War II was a "woman's war" being fought "so that no woman anywhere shall have to be a slave to a Fascist State which makes her no more than a brood mare."

Media messages about women's worth being related first and foremost to family continued into the 1950's. While guilt was manipulated during the war to encourage women to work harder at their jobs, guilt was used after the war against women who worked outside their homes, whether they did so by choice or by necessity.

### Media's Message Today

Today, unemployment is a growing problem in the United States economy. Opinion-makers, including the "moral majority," suggest to women through the media that women's rightful place is in the home and that rigid sex roles are biologically and even divinely determined. This propaganda, however, ignores the many women whose economic position leaves them no choice about working and diminishes the important historical role that women have always played in the economic development of the nation.

Although the crisis of World War II opened the door to expanded definitions of sex roles, at the same time the war fostered a momentum to strengthen traditional roles. When wartime social upheaval created social insecurities, many people turned to the family, and within it to familiar male and female roles, for institutional stability.

The working experience of American women during the war had shown that women were versatile enough to do heavy industrial labor normally considered men's work. By the end of the war, however, that versatility was no longer useful. In fact, it was seen to threaten the status quo, especially when industry no longer wanted to employ women who had been trained during the wartime emergency.

After the war, women were excluded from the kinds of work they had been doing and pushed back to less desirable jobs or out of the labor market entirely. Retaining their wartime gains proved impossible in the post-war economy, and powerful wartime and post-war propaganda helped orchestrate this defeat.

> I think they prepare women psychologically for whatever role the society wants at that particular time for them to play. After losing so many men, America wanted babies. And we wanted babies. That's ok. But we gave up everything for that. We gave up everything.
> —Lola Weixel, welder

*In the first script excerpt from* Wanted: Women War Work-ers, *a recruitment film produced by the Office of War Information, a narrator urges women to go to work in war plants and implies that idle factory machines are causing the deaths of American soldiers on the battlefronts.*

*The propaganda message in the excerpt from* Women of Steel, *produced later by the same agency, tells middle-class women that it is their patriotic duty to take war jobs, which are no more difficult than familiar housework tasks at home. These jobs in industry, however, clearly belong to the soldiers who will be returning one day to claim them.*

**Wanted: Women War Workers**

[*Musical fanfare, fading behind male voice*] Women are wanted for war production work here in our city. Why? Well, these are our people, safe, secure. Yes, our city is a safe city, now, but so was London, once, and then this happened!

[*Somber music rises, then fades behind voice*] And this can happen right here where we live. It will happen unless we keep America free from invasion, unless we speed up production, unless we speed it up right here in our city.

But it takes human power to keep war factories going, and much of our manpower is going to war. More and more men are being called into the armed forces. Their jobs must be filled—and filled now. And who can fill them? You! You women, you're the ones who must fill them, who can give our boys what they need. [*Music surges*] A thousand more planes, and more and more tanks.[*Explosions*] More and more guns, and more ships.

But there are idle machines in our city's war factories, and they threaten our future security, but more than that, our idle machines will be paid for in death. [*Explosions*] In the death of American boys, our own boys. Your son, your brother, your sweetheart, the boy on the next block. They will pay with their lives for these idle machines. The cas-ualties, the dead, wounded, and missing will be evidence of vacant places on our city's production lines. Vacant places that you women *could* fill.

**"Their jobs must be filled now. And who can fill them? You! You women."**

You women could fill these places, you can run these machines. English women have done it for three years. American women are now doing it all over the country. They're operating drills, they're sewing wing fabrics for army and navy planes, and they're doing delicate assembly work. And *get this*, the women of our town are needed to fill jobs right here. This is a crowded city, we can't take care of any more outsiders [migrating war workers]. War work is interesting, and it's not hard. What's more, you'll know you're helping to win the war and save lives. Most war jobs are as simple as operating the appliances you use in your home. And any woman who can operate a vacuum cleaner can join these women at this job . . .

But if you need training, you can get it, and it's free. It will help you get ahead on your job. We must win this war, but we can't unless you women take over the jobs that men are leaving. And you're needed right now. Victory and the lives of our own men in uniform depend upon you. They count upon you women to produce the tools of war. [*Dramatic music crescendo*] ☐

### Women of Steel

Steel has rightly been called the sinews of peace and the backbone of war. Behind the guns and tanks and ships and planes are the blast furnaces and open hearths. Tending these furnaces have always stood a breed of men apart, giants in the land, those men of steel. [*Music*]

But with our country in peril, the women of America rally in support of their men, and here in this almost-the-last great industry we thought could be handled only by men, these mothers, wives, and sweethearts came to stand shoulder to shoulder with them in almost every capacity. [*Music*] These marvelous women of America. These women of steel.

Of course, we had long since accepted their aptitude in fabrication, the quick sure dexterity of their fingers as in this stainless steel rim assembly. Their adaptability to small tools. But as the need grew for more and more production

GREAT GIRL, MARY PURDUE!

SHE'S A CHAMPION PARACHUTE MAKER!

JOIN HER EVERY MORNING IN

*Wheat Sparkies for Breakfast!*

*Ellen Kaiper Collection, Oakland*

# War, Women and Lipstick—

*by* **CONSTANCE LUFT HUHN**
**Head of the House of Tangee**

*A recent portrait of
Constance Luft Huhn
by Maria de Kammerer*

For the first time in history woman-power is a factor in war. Millions of you are fighting and working side by side with your men.

In fact, you are doing double duty—for you are still carrying on your traditional "woman's" work of cooking, and cleaning, and home-making. Yet, somehow, American women are still the loveliest and most spirited in the world. The best dressed, the best informed, the best looking.

It's a reflection of the free democratic way of life that you have succeeded in keeping your femininity —even though you are doing man's work!

If a symbol were needed of this fine, independent spirit—of this courage and strength—I would choose a lipstick. It is one of those mysterious little essentials that have an importance far beyond their size or cost.

A woman's lipstick is an instrument of personal morale that helps her to conceal heartbreak or sorrow; gives her self-confidence when it's badly needed; heightens her loveliness when she wants to look her loveliest.

No lipstick—ours or anyone else's—will win the war. But it symbolizes one of the reasons why we are fighting...the precious right of women to be feminine and lovely—under any circumstances.

*The Tangee Satin-Finish Lipstick of your choice will keep your lips smoother... longer! It will bring an exclusive grooming and a deep glowing "life" to your lips that defy both time and weather.*

**BEAUTY**—*glory of woman...*

**LIBERTY**—*glory of nations...*

*Protect them both...*

**BUY WAR BONDS AND STAMPS**

**TANGEE** *Lipsticks*

**WITH THE NEW
SATIN-FINISH**

In order to sell more products, advertisers developed unusual connections between luxury goods and the nation's rationale for fighting.
*Photoplay*, September 1943

of the basic metal itself, more loyal women with a dash of true American pluck and adventuresomeness edged further and further into the real work of steel-making.

Some, with a scientific bent, went into metallurgical control and research labs. Girls fresh from chemical engineering school. Old women who had been technical librarians. Emmy Lou Spilane, a college girl, now makes tests of the steel as it comes from the furnaces.

Isn't it pretty hot for you, Miss?

"Well, I hear it gets kind of hot around a kitchen stove, too."

Well, I never thought of that.

"Yes, and it gets pretty hot out there in the South Pacific."

Yes, I see what you mean . . .

Women make good drivers, too. American girls raised to drive the family car have no trouble at all handling trucks and tractors. Edith Stoner's husband is in Alaska. She took this job for the duration. . .

How do you like your job, Mrs. Stoner?

"I love it."

How about after the war. Are you going to keep on working?

"I should say not. When my husband comes back, I'm going to be busy at home."

Good for you! [*Music*]

Here is the office of the supervisor of women employees. She can tell us more about these women of steel. If you will, Mrs. Cambell.

"Women in steel are simply the result of realistic thinking. In time of war, you have to have steel, and you also have to have people to make it. With the Army taking men by the thousands, more than 16,000 from our plants so far, we had to find people to replace them. A great untapped reserve was women. . . ."

Many of our girls have never worked before, outside of our own homes. I've seen the share-the-ride cars picking them up. We have the wives of college professors, club girls, home

*U.S. government recruitment poster*

The daily reality of women's work in war industries was unlike the glamorous picture portrayed in government newsreels.
*National Archives*

girls who are doing it as their patriotic duty. And they all average more than 10 percent in [buying] war bonds. Of course, we have made the plants attractive for them. The women have their own lockers and wash rooms. They come out from work looking like business girls on vacation, really. These girls are thimblers on the tank treadline. One had her own beauty parlor, the other was formerly a cigarette girl in a night club. Some of them are like Mrs. Vernata Tallon, who used to run a record and music store. And Miss Lee Dunning, who now welds on landing barges.

Lee, what did you used to do?

"Believe it or not, I was a baby nurse."

Well, quite a change to this.

"Yeah, but the hours are much shorter."

What do you do with your spare time?

"Recently, I've been interested in the Red Cross blood bank. I've signed up for my fifth contribution."

And what about after this war, Lee?

"Well, this job belongs to some soldier, and when he comes back, he can have it."

Oh, that's swell . . . .

And that gives you an idea of the spirit here. These women are working around the clock, around the calendar. They do a man's job and they can draw a man's pay. And they're doing it safely. They're safer here than in their own homes. [*Music*] All America salutes its Women of Steel. ☐

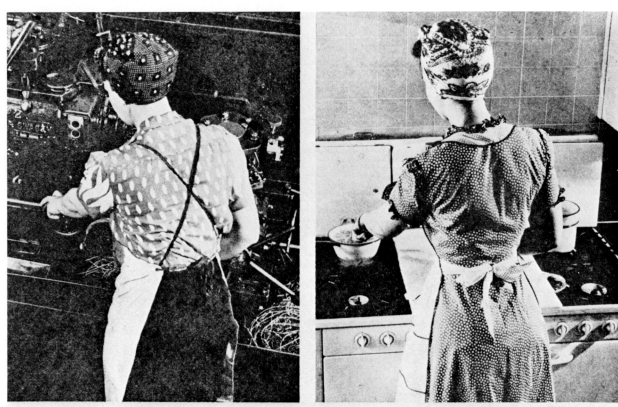

Sisters under the apron—Yesterday's war worker becomes today's housewife.

# What's Become of Rosie the Riveter?

*Ellen Kaiper Collection, Oakland*

# APPENDIX

# FILM SUMMARY

*The Life and Times of Rosie Riveter* is an interchange between the words and images of World War II newsreels and government recruitment films, photographs, and documents on one side and the real-life testimony of five women who worked in war production factories on the other. As the movie progresses, the differences between the myth of the official version of women's work in the war effort and the reality of the personal recollections of the five women who share their experiences become increasingly apparent.

To the strains of the popular 1940's tune, "Rosie the Riveter," the film introduces Wanita Allen, former foundry worker from Detroit; Gladys Belcher, former welder from Richmond, California; Lyn Childs, former shipburner from San Francisco; Lola Weixel, former welder from Brooklyn; and Margaret Wright, former munitions worker from Los Angeles. As the women describe their lives in Depression-era America and the low-paying jobs available to them, the real economic and social reasons that propelled the women into wartime industrial work become increasingly apparent.

## Recruitment and Training of Women War Workers

December 7, 1941, "A day which shall live in infamy." America's entry into the war is announced in newsreel footage followed by clips from government recruitment films which appeal to women's patriotic sense of duty to work in war plants. "*You* are needed right *now!*" Gladys, Margaret, and Lola then recount how they found their first jobs in industry. "It was like a godsend," exclaims Margaret, "for there you were earning pretty good money."

A barrage of government films claims that "working on a [drill] press is as easy as operating a juice extractor in your own home," and the women discuss how they learned their trades.

Wanita and Lyn talk about the ways wartime employers discriminated against black women during hiring. Wanita describes the disappointment of being trained as a crack riveter but being sent to a dirtier job in the foundry because she was a black woman. Lyn recalls that she was denied a job as an elite shipfitter's helper, but quick thinking and a large measure of bravado made her "the only woman ever to make shell burner" at her shipyard.

## Life on the New Job

New women war workers punch time-clocks and demonstrate their skills with machines, tools, and heavy equipment, as Gladys, Wanita, and Lola warmly reminisce about the joys of "sharing and doing it together. . . . We had a happy attitude about our work."

An actress playing the role of "Supervisor of Women Employees" sweetly claims that women in factories are "safer here than in their own homes." In grim contrast, Gladys and Margaret describe workers being forced to provide their own safety equipment, close personal brushes with danger, and frequent industrial accidents and deaths. A 1944 *New York Times* headline reports 37,600 deaths in industry during less than three years of war, more fatalities than occurred on the front lines before D-Day.

Lola then enthusiastically tells how women in her shop organized a United Electrical Workers local, an action which prompted their employer to lock them out. After a pay differential between white and black women was exposed during an organizing drive ("Talk about cheap," remarks Lola), the successful campaign won an 80 percent raise in wages.

Wanita remembers the pleasures of having money in her pocket for the first time. To Benny Goodman's rendition of "Minnie's in the Money," a series of youthful snapshots of the women in the film conveys a sense of new optimism about their lives. Describing how the strong union at her factory gave her for the first time "some say-so on the job," Margaret remembers how this industrial job, unlike her former position as a domestic servant, brought her friends and daily contact with women like herself.

The plant "supervisor" in a government film talks about the "attractive" facilities in the typical war plant. Wanita, however, remembers how white women balked when black women tried to integrate the showers at River Rouge plant in Michigan, a dispute which was soon straightened out by her black United Auto Workers steward.

After a rendition of the government-issue song, "Don't Be An Absentee," Lola describes the work she did at home after she punched out of the factory. Lyn tells about making the agonizing decision to leave her daughter with her family in the South because she couldn't find child care near her San Francisco shipyard. In contrast, a sugary government feature shows a "typical" all-white child care center where "women can leave their children while they work, confident of the best of care in the most pleasant of surroundings." Wanita, Margaret, and Lola share memories about housework and family chores while working overtime hours. Overlooking the realities of women's "double day," a government film falsely claims, "Women were not accustomed to long hours of hard work," and stridently condemns women's absenteeism as causing the war deaths of American soldiers.

Margaret remembers that women who did not want to work ten-hour days were called "unpatriotic." "[They told us] how dare you talk about not working overtime or not doing more than you were supposed to when our boys were over there dying for us. Not for business, but for *us* they were dying."

Lyn tells about nearly losing her job after angrily turning on a white naval officer who was beating a Filipino worker. Although the shipyard colonel accused her of "communist activity" and wanted to fire her, she was able to keep her job because her co-workers stood by her and refused to let her be fired.

Helen Gusmerotti and Mary Mignogna, employed as car repairmen's helpers at the steel car shop in the Pennsylvania Railroad yards, earned 72¢ per hour in 1943. *Marjory Collins, Library of Congress*

Following a news film showing a ship-launching, Lyn remembers how thrilled she was to work in a shipyard because she produced something tangible. Lola recalls the poignant camaraderie in her welding shop where a black co-worker brightened one gloomy, cold night with a comforting proverb in Yiddish.

### The War Ends and Soldiers Return

In an end-of-the-war newsreel, women workers seem eager to give up their jobs when the veterans return. An ingratiating factory owner assures his female employees that there will be "no unemployment hardships on you" because women will all "return home as you promised to do when you came to work for us." Wanita and Lola reminisce about the victory celebrations in 1945, and crowds dance in the streets. "It was simply marvelous," Lola exclaims.

A War Department film describes returning veterans as "the most capable potential group of workers the nation has ever known," ironically using words applied to the women war workers several short years earlier. With celebrations behind them, the women recall the somber reality of being laid off and pounding the pavement looking for work again.

An optimistic narrator projects that in the healthy post-war economy, veterans will be hired, undeveloped countries will be exploited for raw materials, and great quantities of consumer goods will be manufactured. "All employable men and women shall find post-war jobs." In contrast, news footage shows women waiting in long unemployment lines and the former "Rosies" tell about the frustration of being denied skilled industrial jobs solely because they were women.

A popular post-war doctor offers a pseudo-psychological pronouncement on the negative societal effects of women working outside the home. In counterpoint, Lola, Gladys, Margaret, Lyn, and Wanita, women who needed to earn a living, explain how they finally resigned themselves to the less desirable, low-paying jobs available to them.

The return to peacetime living produced, as Lola observes, "a deluge of babies," and Margaret points out how popular expectations about women's "proper" role changed drastically in the post-war years. Lola concludes:

> I believed and I know lots of women who worked with me believed that we were the new woman. But to America at large, while they may have known what our contribution was to the production of this country, we were largely a joke.
>
> And I think that they prepare women psychologically for whatever role the society feels at a particular point they want her to play. After losing so many men, America wanted babies. And we wanted babies, but we gave up everything for that. We gave up everything. □

# Resources for Future Programs

## Books

*In Focus, A Guide to Using Films,* by Linda Blackaby, Dan Georgakas and Barbara Margolis. New York, Zoetrope. Order from Cine-Information, 419 Park Avenue South, New York City, N.Y.

How to incorporate films into organizational education, with advice on operating projectors, developing publicity, and leading discussion groups. Resource lists and readable text make this handbook indispensable.

*Film Programmer's Guide to 16mm Rentals,* by Kathleen Weaver. Reel Research, Box 6037, Albany, CA 94706.

A complete listing of feature and short films with information about distribution and rental, production details, and content. 13,000 titles are listed.

*Reel Change: A Guide to Social Issue Films,* ed. by Patricia Peyton. The Film Fund, P.O. Box 909, San Francisco, CA 94101.

Social issue media, especially films, are listed here, with distribution information, and programming tips.

## Film Libraries

Public libraries, university media centers, museums, union headquarters, religious organizations, and special interest groups lend films from their collections for educational showings at nominal fees. Write to the education department of your organization, or check with your local public library about holdings.

## 16 mm. Films

**Iris Films,** Box 5353, Berkeley, CA 94705. Tel. (415) 549-3192. Distributes films made by women about women, with emphasis on social change. Recommended titles include:

*Good Day Care: One Out of Ten* —Canadian documentary examining contemporary issues in history of day care.

*Ironing*—An interpretation of Tillie's Olsen's story, "I Stand Here Ironing." Working woman reflects on her responsibilities as a mother, including memories of World War II years. Good discussion provoker.

**New Day Films**, Box 315, Franklin Lakes, N.J., 07417. Tel. (201) 891-8240. Cooperative distributes films about women and about occupational health and safety. Recommended titles include:

*Union Maids*—Three women union organizers recall joys and struggles of CIO movement in Chicago in 1930's.

*With Babies and Banners*—Story of General Motors Sit Down Strike in Flint, Michigan, in 1937. Women's Emergency Brigade displayed courage on picket lines, in strike kitchens, and in plant take-over.

*Quilts in Women's Lives*—Documentary portraits of seven quiltmakers who practice this traditional women's art form.

*Song of the Canary*—Critical investigation of deadly health hazards in workplace, with attention to chemical and textile industries.

*Love it Like a Fool*—Features songwriter and performer Malvina Reynolds' life and works. A welder in World War II, Malvina raised her voice for many freedom movements.

**Newsreel,** 630 Natoma Street, San Francisco, 94103. Tel. (415) 621-6196. Distributes films on social and political issues, with emphasis on current labor problems. Recommended releases include:

*The Willmar 8*—Eight women in small Minnesota town begin first bank strike in state's history, picketing through two cold winters for better wages and equal job opportunities.

*The Detroit Model*—Examines current crisis in auto industry through interviews with autoworkers on production lines and in unemployment lines.

*Taylor Chain*—Documents tensions of negotiations, strike votes, and International-local conflicts in a steelworker union local.

*Controlling Interest*—Explores effects of multinational corporate expansion on lives of U.S. and third world workers, and utilizes interviews with corporate executives who support runaway shops and fascist dictatorships as part of "business as usual."

### Other Recommended Films

The following 16mm feature films and labor history documentaries are also good for organizational and educational programming.

*Bound for Glory* (1976)—Feature-length biography of prolific radical folksong writer and performer Woody Guthrie whose famous songs include "This Land is Your Land" and "So Long, It's Been Good to Know You." Contact UA 16, 729 Seventh Ave., New York, NY 10019. Tel. (800) 223-0933.

*Free Voice of Labor* (1980)—Sixty-minute documentary about early 1900's Jewish Labor Anarchists, and contemporary interviews with surviving publishers of anarchist newspapers in New York. Contact Pacific St. Films, 280 Clinton St., Brooklyn, NY 11201. Tel. (212) 875-9722.

*Harlan County, USA* (1977)—Feature-length documentary of coal miners' struggles in "Bloddy" Harlan County, Kentucky. Community women play key role in supporting strike. Contact Cinema 5, 1500 Broadway, New York, NY 10036. Tel. (212)354-5515.

*The Inheritance* (1964)—Sixty-minute documentary about turn-of-the-century union organizing in New York's immigrant communities, especially in the clothing industry. CIO organizing in 1930's also depicted. Contact Amalgamated Clothing and Textile Workers' Union Film Library, 15 Union Square, New York, NY 10003. Tel. (212) 242-0700.

*Nine to Five* (1980)—Comic treatment of contemporary office life from clerical workers' point of view. Contact Films Inc., 5625 Hollywood Blvd., Hollywood, CA. 90028. Tel. (213)466-5481.

*Norma Rae* (1979)—Dramatic story of successful union organizing drive in southern textile mill focusing on one woman's courageous social and personal transformation. Contact Films Inc., 5625 Hollywood Blvd., Hollywood, CA 90028. Tel. (213) 466-5481.

*The Pajama Game* (1957)—Negotiations and shop floor organizing are background of musical comedy set in garment factory in 1950's. Contact Audio Brandon, 7328 San Fernando Road, Sun Valley, CA 91352. Tel. (800) 232-2006 (California) or (800) 423-2590 (U.S.).

*Salt of the Earth* (1952)—Heroic story of miners' strike in New Mexico, including struggle between whites and chicano's and involvement of miners' wives in winning the strike. Contact Audio Brandon, 7838 San Fernando Road, Sun Valley, CA 91352. Tel. (800) 232-2006 (in California) or (800) 423-2590 (U.S.).

*Silver Wings and Santiago Blue* (1980)—Sixty-minute documentary of women military pilots who shuttled planes from aircraft factories to military bases during World War II. Contact Kitty King, 871 Dolly Madison Blvd., McClean, VA 22101. Tel. (703)356-5439.

*The Wobblies* (1979)—Feature length documentary describing colorful history of the radical Industrial Workers of the World (IWW or "Wobblies") who organized unskilled workers before World War I under the banners "One Big Union" and "Abolish the Wage System." Contact First Run Features, 419 Park Ave. South, New York, NY. Tel. (212) 685-6262.

## Slide/Tape Shows

*Community Media Productions*, 215 Superior Avenue, Dayton, OH 45406. Tel. (513) 223-8229.
Distributes slide/tape shows on work and community issues. Recommended titles include:

*We Will Not Be Moved*—Examines displacement of residents in Cincinnati working-class neighborhood that is being "revitalized."
*Why Aren't You Smiling?*—Historical review of women as clerical workers, with emphasis on today's working conditions. ☐

**WITH BABIES and BANNERS:**
Story of the Women's Emergency Brigade

PRESENTED BY: THE WOMEN'S LABOR HISTORY FILM PROJECT
DIRECTOR: LORRAINE GRAY
PRODUCERS: ANNE BOHLEN, LYN GOLDFARB, LORRAINE GRAY
Available from:
NEW DAY FILMS P.O. Box 315, Franklin Lakes, N. J. 07417    (201) 891-8240

From the 1978 documentary, *With Babies and Banners*, the story of the 1930's CIO organizing drive in the auto industry.

# Books for Further Reading

*Wartime Women: Sex Roles, Family Relations and the Status of Women in World War II,* by Karen Anderson. New Britain, Connecticut, Greenwood, 1981.

A scholarly study of women's lives during World War II covering all aspects of the homefront, from childcare and rationing to wartime industrial recruitment, union activity and postwar "reconversion." Anderson's exhaustive study supplements the issues raised in the film.

*The Dollmaker,* by Harriet Arnow. New York, MacMillan, 1949.

A beautiful, intense novel about family life in a workers' housing project in Detroit during the war. The story centers around Gertie Nevels, who has left Kentucky with her children and how she grapples with urban "adjustment."

*America's Working Women, A Documentary History,* edited by Rosalyn Baxandall, Linda Gordon and Susan Reverby. New York, Vintage Books, 1976.

An excellent, broad collection of historical articles from 1600 to the present, including important first-person narratives of World War II industrial experiences and statistics.

*I Looked Over Jordon,* by Ernie Brill. Boston, South End Press, 1980.

A series of stories about hospital worklife, as observed by a humorous orderly. The title story is a gripping and beautifully told narrative of the effects of white lung disease (as-bestos poisoning) on a retired Richmond, California, shipyard worker.

*The American Woman: Her Changing Social, Economic and Political Role, 1920-1970,* by William H. Chafe. New York, Oxford University Press, 1972.

A broad historical study of women in the U.S. after suffrage with two excellent descriptive chapters on women workers in World War II.

*Indignant Heart, A Black Worker's Journal,* by Charles Denby. Boston, South End Press, 1978.

Memoirs of Southern migration and industrial and community organizing by a black militant worker-writer whose experiences include the Detroit riots of 1943 and the uprising of 1967. Political struggles within the unions and in the South are all described in vivid detail.

*Songs of Work and Protest,* by Edith Fowke and Joe Glazer. New York, Dover Publications, 1973.

One hundred classic American folk/labor songs are anthologized with words, melody lines, and background notes. They provide a combination of labor and cultural history and make possible enjoyable group sing-along activities.

*All the Livelong Day,* by Barbara Garson. New York, Penguin, 1974.

A subjective but thoroughly fascinating trip through the small shops and oppressive offices of metropolitan New York City where millions of women workers fight alienation, mismanagement and the deadening power of routine. Their "weapons" are occasionally unions, but more often their own frail relationships with each other.

*Wartime Strikes,* by Martin Glaberman. Detroit, Bewick Ed., 1979.

A study documenting the instances, reasons for, and reactions to numerous "wildcats" that took place in World War II industrial workplaces, and the role of the CIO's no-strike pledge in transforming labor-management relations in the 1940's.

*Separated and Unequal: Discrimination Against Women Workers after World War II,* by Lyn Goldfarb. Union of Radical Political Economics, pamphlet, Washington, D.C., 1976.

A study detailing discriminatory layoffs and the use of separate seniority lists during reconversion in United Auto Worker locals, with extensive documentary quotes from case histories.

*From Reverence to Rape: The Treatment of Women in the Movies,* by Molly Haskell. New York, Penguin, 1974.

A feminist analysis of the image of women in films, with chapters on women in World War II feature films.

*Women and Work,* ed. by Florence Howe. Old Westbury, Feminist Press, 1978.

A thorough collection of poetry, fiction and essays about the work experience of women. Good variety of historical and contemporary materials with excellent discussion potential.

*Pink Collar Workers: Inside the World of Women's Work,* by Louise Kapp Howe. New York, Putnam, 1977.

A study of the "pink collar ghetto" of women's low wage, dead-end jobs, with special emphasis on clerical and restaurant work in the United States.

*Working Women Roots, An Oral History Primer,* ed. by Joyce Kornbluh. Ann Arbor, Institute of Labor and Industrial Relations, 1979.

A step-by-step guide on how to collect women's labor history, with sample transcripts.

*Black Women in White America: A Documentary History,* ed. by Gerda Lerner. New York, Vintage, 1973.

An important and exhaustive historical anthology of black women's heritage in America from the days of slavery through the 1960's. Excellent accounts of union drives in the twentieth century and thorough materials on political, educational, and economic struggles for survival.

"Organizing the Sexual Division of Labor: Historical Perspectives on 'Women's Work' and the American Labor Movement," by Ruth Milkman, in *Socialist Review,* January, 1980.

A critical review of the experiences of women workers in U.S. trade union organizing history, with a look at what needs to be done now that unorganized workers comprise the major portion of the female workforce.

*Black Detroit and the Rise of the UAW,* by August Meier and Elliott Rudwick. New York, Oxford, 1979.

An exhaustive historical analysis of race relations in the auto plants, focusing on the war years. The links between CIO unions, the black community and the industry itself are explored in careful detail, illuminating World War II's transformational influence on black history.

*The Films of World War II,* by Joe Morella, Edward Z. Epstein, and John Griggs. Secaucus, Citadel, 1973.

Almost 100 World War II Hollywood productions are catalogued and reviewed with illustrative production stills. Photographs of pin-up girls and summary essays describing the involvement of the office of War Information in feature film production tell the story behind the films that accompanied "March of Time" newsreels and propaganda shorts in commercial theaters.

*Mobilizing Women for War: German and American Propaganda, 1939-45,* by Leila J. Rupp. Princeton, Princeton Press, 1978.

A study documenting and analyzing German and American propaganda aimed at women defense industry workers with special and insightful attention to the connections between ideology, public policy and mass media manipulation.

*Displaced Homemakers,* by Laurie Shields. New York, McGraw Hill, 1981.

A study focusing on the pragmatic (and dramatic) efforts of widowed and divorced women considered "too old" for the job market to secure funding for training and to build group organization as well as dynamic personal change. Good listings of readings and organizations.

*Labor Education for Women Workers,* ed. by Barbara Wertheimer. Philadelphia, Temple University Press, 1980.

A thorough and useful anthology of essays on developing programs for women workers in stewardship skills, political action, labor/oral history, and occupational health and safety. Indispensable for union educators.

*We Were There: The Story of Working Women in America,* by Barbara Wertheimer. New York, Pantheon Press, 1977.

Details the history of women's work experiences in the United States in a lively narrative style with illustrations. Good basic background in labor history.

*What Really Happened to Rosie the Riveter—Demobilization and the Female Labor Force, 1944-47,* by Sheila Tobias and Lisa Anderson, New York, Pantheon Press, 1977.

An analysis of post-war dismissals of women defense workers, emphasizing the forcible layoffs of women who wanted and needed to work. The UAW's role in reconversion is especially examined.

*Radical America,* Volume 9, nos. 4-5. Cambridge, Massachusetts, 1975.

A special issue on American labor in the 1940's includes analyses of the no-strike pledge in CIO organizing, personal narratives by women workers, and a bibliographical essay.

*Bargaining for Equality,* by the Women's Labor Project, San Francisco, 1981.

A legal handbook for organizers, negotiators, and advocates of women's rights in unions. Pragmatic information on child care, job-sharing, affirmative action, and sexual harassment. ☐